Hawking Ground Quarry

Hawking Ground Quarry

Martin Hollinshead

hancock

house

ISBN 0-88839-320-2

Copyright © 1993 Martin Hollinshead

Cataloging in Publication Data
Hollinshead, Martin, 1959–
    Hawking ground quarry

ISBN 0-88839-320-2

1. Falconry.   2. Ferreting.   I. Title.
SK321.H64 1993   799.2'32   C93-091400-7

Edited: Herb Bryce, Myron Shutty
Production: Lorna Lake

Published simultaneously in Canada and the United States by

HANCOCK HOUSE PUBLISHERS LTD.
19313 Zero Avenue, Surrey, B.C. V4P 1M7
(604) 538-1114   Fax (604) 538-2262

HANCOCK HOUSE PUBLISHERS
1431 Harrison Avenue, Box 959, Blaine, WA 98231
(206) 354-6953   Fax (604) 538-2262

Contents

Preface

If one discounts fishing, then falconry was my introduction to field sports. Actually, falconry is far too grand a word to describe my early boyhood activities, for we (I shared my interest with a school friend) never took to the fields with anything more rapacious than a kestrel or common buzzard. I recall our ambitious plans for 'Buzz' and how we hoped she might one day make a rabbit hawk. She never did, but then two young would-be falconers and an overweight buzzard is hardly a recipe for success. But try we did, and those early thwarted attempts must have stirred something in me, for today I am still out there pursuing rabbits—with slightly more positive results, I might add.

It's strange, but I have never had any desire to hunt anything other than mammalian quarries and although I have not restricted myself to rabbit hawking, all of the quarries I have pursued with any seriousness have been furred rather than feathered.

This has led me to concentrate on flying those raptors which, in Europe, one tends to associate with ground quarries, such as goshawks, *Buteos*, and golden eagles.

I consider myself lucky in that I have been able to travel a little and fly hawks in a number of different countries.

This has been of immeasurable benefit to my falconry. The years I spent in Germany (then West Germany) influenced me greatly as did, in a more immediate sense, my first hawking trips into eastern Europe, these being at a time when eastern Europe was quite isolated from the West. And continental falconry continues to be an influence, as I spend part of each season hawking with friends in these very same areas.

When I first considered writing a book on hawking, I had but one thought in mind and that was to write only about the hunting side of things. It seemed to me that the basics had been discussed often enough, and to go over such well-trodden ground again would be pointless. I simply could not bring myself to write of jesses, bells, perches, etc. If I did, I felt sure, the reader would find my descriptions of such items just as tedious to read as I had found them to write.

This book covers most aspects of hawking ground quarry but I have elected not to discuss the use, or possible use, of bagged game. In some countries, bagged game is a legitimate and acceptable part of falconry; but in many parts of Europe, field sports in general are under so much pressure from those who would see all kinds of hunting banned, I felt it wise to avoid the topic.

One of my main concerns was how the book would be illustrated. Being aware of my own literary limitations, I feared that words alone would not suffice if I were to capture the essence of the true hawking experience. I was not so worried about dealing with the more familiar topics such as rabbit hawking with goshawks and *Buteos,* but the thought of writing about hunting with golden eagles without the right kind of photographic support was very unappealing. Luckily, friend and expert photographer Dieter Kuhn came to my aid. In fact, if it had not been for Dieter's skill with a camera and his willingness to get involved, I think I

7

would have been considerably less enthusiastic about the whole project.

Now that the book is finished, I hope it will be evaluated for what it is rather than be judged for what it is not. It was never my intention to write some kind of grand or definitive work on hawking. This is quite simply a small book about the practical side of hunting with hawks. It is my humble tribute to a sport which has given me so very much.

MARTIN HOLLINSHEAD

1   The Goshawk

Taking Europe as a whole, the goshawk, *Accipiter gentilis,* must easily be the most widely utilized bird of the chase. In countries such as Germany, Austria, Hungary, and the area formerly known as Czechoslovakia, *gentilis* is extremely highly regarded as a game-catching hawk, and in these countries a high degree of excellence has been achieved with this species.

In Britain, the situation is somewhat different; while the goshawk is certainly very popular, it does have competition. This competition comes in the form of the red-tailed buzzard and the Harris' hawk, for these two New World species might prove more appealing to the hunter of ground quarries than a female gos. A small number of red-tails and Harris' hawks are flown on the continent, but they in no way threaten the goshawk's prominent position.

One of the reasons some British falconers have sought an alternative to the gos is its notoriously difficult temperament. I believe that many falconers, having been forewarned, never actually consider the goshawk as a hunting companion and go immediately for a less troublesome bird.

This is a great pity, for, although *gentilis* certainly does have a difficult side to its nature, as an all-round hunting hawk it really is in a class of its own. In skilled hands, nothing will touch it.

As a hunting bird in the field, the goshawk's ability is truly amazing, and it is little wonder that early Asian falconers rated it so highly. In the past, Japanese falconers hunted geese and cranes with goshawks; feats of this nature demonstrate not only a high degree of skill on the falconer's part, but also show just what the goshawk is capable of.

With such a bird, the modern falconer has a multitude of quarry options open to him. Indeed, it would probably be easier to list the quarries that definitely cannot be taken with a trained gos than those which might be. In Europe, the more normal quarries include: rabbits, hares, squirrels, pheasants, ducks, and partridge. However, depending on the falconer's skill and ingenuity, all manner of game can be brought to bag. For example, rooks feeding in roadside fields make an interesting and worthwhile flight for a gos being slipped from a car window.

At least eight subspecies of northern goshawk have been described, and three of these (*A. g. atricapillus, A. g. laingi, A. g. apache*) are found in North America. The North American birds are quite different to those from the Old World, and it has been suggested that they might be a separate species. A very striking subspecies is *A. g. albidus* of northeastern Siberia and Kamchatka. This is a very pale goshawk with some individuals being almost totally white. They are larger birds than those of central Europe, but not as large as *A. g. buteoides* of extreme northern Scandinavia. In Siberia, *A. g. buteoides'* range lies west of that occupied by *A. g. albidus*.

10

Rabbit Hawking with Goshawks

The rabbit, unlike the hare, is not a native British mammal. Its appearance in Britain has been linked with the Romans by some authorities, while others favor a Norman connection. There is, in fact, strong evidence to suggest that the rabbit's introduction should indeed be attributed to the Normans, who, it is believed, first brought these animals to Britain shortly after the conquest. These 'Norman' rabbits were kept in enclosed warrens and farmed for their meat and fur. Inevitably, some individuals absconded and became established beyond the warrens. So began the rabbit's colonization of Britain.

The rabbit has long been a valued falconry quarry in Britain. In fact, when *myxomatosis* all but wiped out the rabbit population in the 1950s, active hawking was dealt a colossal blow. Almost overnight, the single most important goshawk quarry practically disappeared. Thankfully the rabbit is once again found in substantial numbers and today British falconry relies very heavily indeed on this animal.

Goshawks are extremely well suited to rabbit hawking; although it must be emphasized that females are much more desirable than males. Some central European males will take rabbits, but they are rarely as effective as their larger sisters. The problem with male goshawks lies not in catching rabbits but in holding them. Rabbit hawking with a male is a little like hare hawking with a female—things tend to get physical! Female goshawks can be truly deadly with rabbits and normally have little difficulty in controlling them. Having said that, I always make a point of getting to the bird as quickly as possible for, depending on how and where she has taken her victim, there is still a chance of its struggling free.

One of the best rabbiting goshawks I have ever seen perform belonged to a German friend. This bird, a wild-taken eyas, displayed many undesirable imprint traits and was so vocal that she frequently ended up locked in the car, which was then put away in the garage. She could certainly be a bit of a burden at home, but out in the field her performance was awe inspiring. This bird's almost super-natural ability impressed all who saw her hunt, and she earned quite a reputation for herself and her owner.

In Germany, much of my rabbit hawking was done in the company of friends and, I might add, in some pretty odd places. A regular venue was the 'quieter' side of a huge rubbish dump. Compared to that, the inner-city parks we also hawked were a real treat. The authorities had given us permission to hunt in these municipal rabbit strongholds, and we always enjoyed plenty of sport. Yet, in such sur-roundings, with the goshawks dodging either piles of junk or joggers, the overall hawking experience was hardly a fulfilling one. Because of this, I have to confess to fre-quently hawking alone in far more attractive locations, where my presence was perhaps a little less legitimate. Not far from where I lived at the time was a vast German military training area and it was there that I would hawk.

Hawking at the training area was difficult. Problems came from two directions. First, the terrain itself which was heavily wooded, often in huge unbroken tracts, and hilly. Second, there was a very real need for me not to be seen or heard. Dogs and ferrets were out and the birds themselves (I flew two goshawks there at different times) needed to be nonvocal. A noisy hawk could really have given the game away.

On hawking days my procedure was always the same. I would drive the narrow snaking lane to the training area, pull off using some forest track and park, or should I say hide, the car. Then, after checking if the coast was clear, the gos would be discretely removed from its transport box and we would disappear into the cover of the trees. Once away from the car, I felt a good deal better.

Generally speaking, I never saw a living soul during my secret trips, these being conducted on nonexercise days; but on a couple of occasions, I did have close calls with the military. I remember coming up behind a group of soldiers who were dug into fox holes. They were so well hidden I nearly walked straight in amongst them. Luckily, I realized my mistake just in time and managed to sneak off, hawk on hand, unseen.

The hawking itself was quite varied. The area was extensive and changed in character as one moved through it. In some places flights from the fist were necessary, in other spots the bird needed to be given a lot more freedom. I certainly enjoyed some fine sport but gradually became overconfident. Not overconfident hawking wise (this is something the terrain would not allow) but in my ability to come and go unseen as I pleased. Because of this, one winter my excursions were brought to an abrupt end.

A couple of days prior to the incident I had been out early after a light fall of fresh snow. With no ferrets to fall back on, the morning had been pretty poor and uneventful. However, I did manage to track a rabbit across a woodland bank to its resting place in a bit of cover alongside a fallen tree. The rabbit was poked out and taken by the hawk (being flown from the fist) as it entered the bottom of a bush. As flights go, it was about as straightforward as they come but it had been quite interesting tracking the rabbit and it was the thought of repeating the performance that took me back to the same general area on the fateful day. I parked the car as normal, taking perhaps not as much care as I should have, and made my way to a spot where I hoped there would be sufficient ground cover for me to find a rabbit or two lying out. Again in the snow, rabbit and other animal tracks were abundant, but it was the less abundant human boot prints that drew my attention. The prints were fresh and right then I should have made a careful retreat but I did not. Instead, I continued my search for rabbits probing likely looking spots and observing tracks, totally unaware that from a distance I too, was being scrutinised and observed. If the bootprints in the snow were a warning then the bird's behavior should have set alarm bells ringing. She did not become restless as such but it was obvious she had spotted something and it was definitely not quarry. Nevertheless, try as I did, I couldn't see anything out of the ordinary. Carrying on, I continued my quest for rabbits oblivious to the fact that I was being stalked by some figure in the forest. So engrossed was I that the large official-looking and heavily armed gentleman got within about thirty yards of me before I saw him. I won't go into the details of what happened but suffice to say my wanderings through the military's woodland were over.

Woodland rabbit hawking takes some beating, but it is not always an ideal pastime for the novice or faint at heart (even when everything is legitimate and above board). The general idea is to flush rabbits under or close to the hawk; but if rabbits (or other possible quarries) are abundant and the gos is being flown from the high treetops, then things can easily get out of hand. From her lofty position, the hawk might spot a rabbit 'sneaking off' some way ahead. Her attack is launched and she is quickly an uncomfortably long distance away. Having missed on the first attempt, she throws up into another tree and from this vantage point she again quickly catches a fleeting glimpse of quarry and she's off again. The best the falconer can do is to try to keep up. If the hawk kills in the ground cover, she might prove difficult to find; and a badly taken rabbit can sometimes pull a hawk into the most unlikely places. I remember one gos being dragged under a dense mat of damp leaves, which perfectly concealed both her and her quarry.

Not every woodland hawking experience with goshawks need be a nerve-racking one. If one chooses small, isolated woods and makes a point of familiarizing oneself with the layout, some truly excellent sport can be had. However, before commencing, one will need to wait until most of the leaves have fallen. Otherwise, keeping sight of the hawk as she flies among the branches can prove difficult.

Unfortunately, if one does much woodland work, goshawks tend to become rather independent; but, when rabbits are available only in woodland settings, one will have to suffer this inconvenience. Naturally, one always keeps a lure of some description at hand. Good bells are essential and telemetry advisable.

When hawking through woodland, a slow and steady approach is required. Every rabbity looking spot must be checked meticulously. There is absolutely no need to go madly thrashing and crashing about. All this tends to do is flush rabbits out of range, and in an uncontrolled manner. With this in mind, overenthusiastic beaters are best left at home. I must confess that I prefer to hawk alone in woodland. I enjoy the air of tension and anticipation that is created as I search for quarry in an almost secretive fashion.

Flights to woodland rabbits will vary, depending on the ground cover and tree density. In open woodland containing sparse cover, flights are fairly direct. Any rabbits flushed simply head for home at speed. When the ground cover is thick and extensive and the trees themselves are closely grouped, then hawking rabbits is less predictable and really far more enjoyable. Under these conditions, rabbits will use the cover to their best advantage, moving certainly but trying never to cross an open space; and that is exactly what the falconer or his dog must force them into doing. For this type of work, a good steady dog is of great value, and the hawk soon learns to interpret its behavior. When hawking in this way, the falconer may see the hawk make several attempts at quarry, but not see a rabbit until one is actually in the bird's feet.

There are two possible hazards to be borne in mind by the woodland rabbit hawker, one man-made, the other natural. The man-made hazard comes in the form of wire perimeter fencing. A rabbit running along or through an old rusty and therefore camouflaged fence can be the undoing of a determined hawk.

The other possible hazard is that tough customer, the gray squirrel. Sooner or later old bushy tail is going to be encountered, and this is one meeting the serious rabbit hawker can do without. While the visual nature of squirrel flights makes them undoubtedly appealing, the thrill of these aerial antics is always tempered by the knowledge that the pursued is capable of seriously injuring the pursuer. A bad squirrel bite can result in permanent foot damage. I have known a squirrel bite to cost a male goshawk one of its toes. Yet, despite the innate risks, some falconers find squirrel hawking irresistible and when rabbits are scarce, one can easily turn to almost any available quarry.

I suppose the simplest form of rabbiting with goshawks is either working hedgerows and other clumps of cover or, for the more optimistic, looking for rabbits lying out in fields. Hedgerows frequently contain rabbit warrens and so there is always a chance of finding a rabbit or two lying in, or alongside, a hedge. Even when there is no actual warren, rabbits can still be found in hedgerows; and often these hedgerow rabbits are a considerable distance from home. Generally speaking, rabbits will not be found lying too far from their warrens during daylight hours, but it's surprising just how far away from any form of true safety some individuals can be located. Rabbits can be walked up in fields, but there will need to be sufficient cover to provide them with enough concealment. There is little point looking for rabbits on a grass field that has been grazed bowling-green smooth by sheep. Rough, tussocky grass fields are a different thing, and here one really does have a chance at finding rabbits; and, more importantly, of finding rabbits far enough away from cover (or their warrens) to provide viable flights. But this type of hawking can prove a very hit-and-miss affair, and the really keen rabbit hawker out for a day's sport and intent on seeing some action will normally have a ferret or two along just in case. Ferreting to a good female gos is excellent sport, and for serious rabbit hawking, I believe ferrets are indispensable. Early in the season one can often find enough rabbits lying out above ground, but to rely on such encounters as winter progresses would be foolhardy.

The most enjoyable way of working ferrets with hawks is when two or three people are out together and one is concentrating solely on the ferrets. To my mind, this is the best method by far, and it certainly makes life easier for those flying the hawks. One can handle things alone if necessary, but my first choice would be for a ferreting companion every time.

When it comes to describing suitable locations for ferreting to goshawks, the task is not an easy one. An experienced bird will take bolted rabbits under some very difficult conditions and, although nice open textbook warrens are always welcome, the goshawker should not be put off by the more challenging options.

Ferreting in woodland can be interesting, and as long as there is not too much ground cover, a gos will really show some sport at bolted woodland rabbits. On a smaller scale but similar theme, isolated pitholes often contain warrens around their inside perimeter, and these, too, deserve consideration. Actually, whether ferreting or not, pitholes supporting trees and other vegetation should not be overlooked. Their location often makes them an oasis in an otherwise flat, featureless expanse of unrabbity country.

Rabbits bolted from hedgerows will also be taken by a goshawk. Ideally one wants fairly narrow and low hedges that allow the hawk to be slipped at rabbits whichever side they bolt. Once persuaded to move, rabbits will often run along a hedge, but, surprisingly enough, at times they will also make a dash straight out across open ground.

Correctly positioning oneself for the slip is vitally important, wherever the warren is situated. Getting too close is a big mistake, and it is one made by no small number of tyros. Their keenness has them all but peering down any possible exit holes in anticipation of the bolt, and they may have a very long wait indeed!

Generally speaking, I try to avoid warrens which give the impression of being extensive. Sites with perhaps half a dozen holes or so would be my first choice and, really, from a positioning point of view, the fewer holes the better. Much really depends on the location itself. A smallish number of closely grouped holes would obviously be given preference over a warren strung out along an old hedge. Of course, just because a warren appears small doesn't necessarily mean that it is. Two or three well-worn surface holes positioned temptingly on some grassy bank might welcome one's ferrets into a cavernous labyrinth.

Hare Hawking with Goshawks

The British Isles are home to three types of hare, the European brown hare, *Lepus capensis,* the blue or mountain hare, *Lepus timidus scoticus,* and the Irish hare, *Lepus timidus hibernicus.* Of the three, the brown hare is the largest, weighing seven to eight pounds and more. Individuals of fourteen pounds have been recorded.

How falconers view the brown hare will largely depend on the type of bird they are flying. With goshawks, the falconer's most serious concern is the quarry's weight and strength. Of course, if given too much 'law,' a fit hare is capable of outdistancing a gos, but if slips are kept short then success in these flights will eventually come down to whether or not the bird can hold its victim once it catches the thing. Actually, much depends on the falconer and how quickly he or she can lend assistance. Haste really is of the utmost importance, as dawdling may result not only in the hare's escape but also a damaged hawk. One must get to the bird as quickly as possible.

Hawking adult brown hares with a goshawk can be a rough business and some of the scenes one witnesses are truly violent with hawk and hare smashing and crashing about all over the place. The most common thing to suffer in such encounters is the hawk's plumage; but the risk of a true injury being sustained should never be ruled out especially when hawking is being conducted over hard ground.

As demanding as this type of hawking is for goshawks, birds which have been specifically prepared for the task, can make effective hare catchers. Nevertheless, due to the physical nature of the flight, many falconers (with other quarry at their disposal) prefer not to pursue hares with their goshawks. I think it could certainly be suggested that in the more typical hare flights, goshawk and hare are not really seen at their best. As a goshawk quarry, the European rabbit can provide for more varied sport.

One tends to think of the brown hare inhabiting mainly open landscapes; however, this big *lagomorph* is also frequently met with in woodland, especially during periods of harsh weather. Some continental authorities actually differentiate between 'field' and 'woodland' hares, and my own observations on the Continent lead me to believe that brown hares do sometimes adopt a woodland existence. My experience is limited to deciduous woodland. I have not found brown hares living in coniferous forests, although this type of habitat does seem acceptable to blue hares in the Scottish border country.

When I think of woodland hares I see, in my mind's eye, a familiar scene. I visualize open broadleafed woodland containing a lot of beech. I see the woodland floor carpeted golden with shed leaves and above this perched on some prominent tree limb, a steely gray adult female goshawk. The landscape the goshawk surveys is an uneven one. It rises and falls in gentle folds. There is no ground cover as such just the odd fallen tree, a bit of brushwood, and a scattering of holly. All is still, but out there somewhere lies a hare sitting tight. Aware of our presence, the tension inside her is building but instinct tells her that at this point concealment is her best course of action. This is soon to change. As I moved on, a dry twig snaps underfoot and the hare takes to her heels. I don't see her to start with but in these dry quiet woods the disturbance caused by her hasty departure is quite audible. Then I spot her but it's only a fleeting glimpse for she soon disappears over a rise; it is here, hidden behind a curtain of holly, that the gos, who was on the wing as soon as the hare first moved, goes in for the kill. The outcome? Well, in this instance, let's leave the hare to make her escape looking larger and more magnificent than ever in this seemingly unnatural setting.

In North America, a true woodland dweller, the snowshoe hare, *Lepus americanus,* provides excellent sport for goshawks. Mr. Kent Christopher, writing in the 1980 edition of the *Welsh Hawking Club Journal,* gives an interesting account of this type of hawking. He writes:

These hares are pure white in the winter and change to brown in the summer. They weigh from 2-4 pounds and are found in swamps, forests and thickets throughout much of northern North America and south along the mountain ranges. They are primarily nocturnal and feed mostly on bark, twigs and buds in winter. They are named for their very large, furry feet which enable them to walk and run on top of light fluffy snow.

To be successful in hunting these hare, the hawk must be taught to take stand high up in a tree. The falconer and if he is lucky enough to have company, begin to move through the frozen swamps and thickets trying for a flush. It would be nearly impossible to hunt snowshoe from the fist since they often run far up ahead and out of sight. It is also difficult to walk through the thick cover and in 3 to 4 feet of snow with a hawk on the fist. Starting from a high perch gives the hawk a tremendous advantage.

Of course, in most cases the hawk is the first to spot the hare and take wing. The falconer does his best to keep up with the action. The hare uses the thick cover and runs through and round the bushes in an effort to escape. We generally get well over 5 meters (200 or more inches) of snow in a season and this provides the hare with numerous snow caves or tunnels in which to take refuge. After a hare runs into a snow tunnel I generally find the hawk standing over the tunnel entrance and at times she even ran down the tunnel after the hare. With the hare in a snow tunnel I generally tried to poke it out with a stick. If that wasn't successful I used a ferret. In either case we usually get a classic goshawk flight through the thick cover.

Once Cynthia took hold of the hare's head it was all over for the big white bunny. With one foot on the head and the other on the hare's back, the hare generally tried to pull loose by digging under the snow. Like all good hares, they try their best to kick free of the hawk with their powerful hind legs. Snowshoes are not the biggest of hares but the fact that they are hunted in the thickest of cover and in deep snow makes them tough quarry indeed. We have had some truly memorable flights and I will always enjoy strapping on a pair of snowshoes and beating through the white winter landscape flushing big white bunnies for a good gos.

2 The Harris' Hawk and the Red-tailed Hawk

In Britain the Harris' hawk, *Parabuteo unicinctus*, and the red-tailed hawk, *Buteo jamaicensis*, have a very strong following indeed; and just why these two birds are so popular is not difficult to fathom. Both are very capable hunting hawks and at the same time are steady and reliable.

The Harris' in particular has become very popular and has influenced British falconry more than any other introduced species. What makes the Harris' so popular is its nature. This accommodating raptor is truly likable. Because of this, it tends to be a firm favorite of the not-so-experienced falconer. In fact, I suspect that the Harris' has allowed a good many people to practice falconry who would never have coped with a goshawk (or perhaps even a redtail). Unfortunately, as the *Parabuteo* seems prepared to do anything short of jump through a hoop for its human partner, it attracts a great many pseudofalconers. This is a pity, for the Harris' deserves to be taken seriously, and really belongs in the hands of a dedicated hunter.

Although the Harris' and red-tail are capable of taking a variety of quarries, including game birds under the right conditions, in Britain they are very much associated with rabbit hawking. As they will perform against rabbits under similar conditions to the goshawk, comparisons are almost unavoidable. Like the gos, both of these broadwings (a term I use loosely for convenience) will fly and hunt in woodland. However, it must be said that under really tight conditions, the gos is more effective. This is especially true if some flights from the fist are required. When pursuing quarry, a hunting goshawk will cut its way through dense woodland with amazing dexterity.

If rabbits are to be walked up in field where ground cover is so sparse that once disturbed they simply make an all-out direct dash for sanctuary, then a good gos will prove a hard act to follow. Much depends on how far the rabbit has to run, but in the shortish sprint so often witnessed under such conditions, the devastating acceleration so typical of accipiters can mean the difference between success and failure.

On the other hand, if rabbits can be located in patchy vegetation some way from true safety, then the broadwings can prove very efficient, especially if the area is dotted with trees.

For general-purpose ferreting over a variety of landscapes, the goshawk has no serious competition. This bird will take bolted rabbits under such hugely diverse conditions that no broadwing could hope to keep pace. Harris' hawks and red-tails will take bolted rabbits, but no one who has fully tested the goshawk's ability at the ferreting game could doubt its superiority.

The red-tail is the larger of the two broadwings and, if correctly trained, females will make very potent hunting hawks and are quite capable of taking hares. Nevertheless, the Harris' is generally considered a better all-rounder.

However, it must be said that for serious rabbit hawking (and I emphasis serious), females of the species should always be considered preferable to males. As with male goshawks from central Europe, some male Harris' will take rabbits, but they are never as deadly as females. The smaller male just has not got the weight to stop strong winter rabbits in their tracks, unless he takes them just right. Here lies the problem, for no matter how skilled the hawk might be, in some instances it will have to take hold of the quarry wherever and however it can, and in such a situation bulk and power count, not technique.

No doubt many falconers will feel I am selling the male Harris' short. This is not my intention at all. I am simply trying to look at things as practically as possible. Yes, male Harris' (especially the heavier individuals) will take rabbits, but an average female will give a better overall performance at this quarry.

In recent years, much of my rabbit hawking has taken place in what I suppose one would term moderately high hill country. This runs up to about 1,700 feet, and on the lower, gently sloping hillsides, rabbits are abundant. Records show that this was, in fact, once the site of an old working warren and although today *myxomatosis* periodically raises its ugly head, there is never any real impact on the rabbit population and one is always guaranteed plenty of sport. Friends and I have flown a variety of birds here, but all seem to agree that a good female Harris' is hard to beat.

The country is well suited to soaring flights, and this is where the Harris' (and red-tail) starts to win back points from the goshawk. Early in the season, a low, patchy carpet of bracken allows rabbits to be walked up on the hillside. Depending on the weather conditions, the Harris' either slope soars or flies from the fist. In practice, one normally sees a little of both. The soaring flights vary, from those which see the bird holding a fairly high position almost directly overhead, to others where she may closely hug the hillside. It much depends on wind conditions and how one is working the ground. This all sounds very casual, but let there be no mistake about it, the hawk is hunting and knows that sooner or later a rabbit will be forced to expose itself. Due to the cover conditions, the success ratio of these flights is not high. Rabbits do get taken, but they are hard earned. However, the flying itself more than compensates for the small bag.

Later in the season, when the elements have bashed and flattened the cover (this normally requires some snow), ferreting is absolutely essential and flights are of a more direct nature. With the cover gone, one starts to appreciate just how suitable this area must be for rabbits. The hillsides are littered with warrens. Under these conditions, the best hawking is seen when one has two or three experienced hawks along and a 'team' of reliable ferrets. The day consists of ferreting and more ferreting; and large numbers of rabbits are bolted. During such days, the male Harris' hawks can really have their work cut out, especially on the more steeply sloping ground. Before it bolts, a rabbit knows exactly where it is going and intends to get there. Out of the warren it rockets off across, or down, the smooth grass hillside. Under these conditions, a determined adult rabbit weighing, shall we say, three and a half pounds, can take some stopping, and a fair old rough and tumble is often seen before the 'bouncing bundle' is brought under control. If the quarry is badly taken, perhaps by a rear leg or its rear end, and is already near to its destination, it might end up pulling the Harris' halfway down a rabbit hole. Actually, more than a few rabbits get bagged this way. One slips a hand past the bird's wings, which will be spread each side of the hole acting as a brace, and searches for the rabbit's legs. Both hawk and rabbit are then extracted.

Some very enjoyable days have been had with mixed groups (Harris', red-tail, goshawk), but two females Harris' that get on well together take some beating. Of course, not all Harris' do get on with others of their own kind, and although this normally gregarious hawk is often quite safe in company, some individuals are extremely antisocial.

Although this hawking is being conducted over sloping, treeless hillsides, the landscape's rather even nature is punctuated with ridges and gullies. Such features make flights less mundane than one might imagine. Add to this the fact that any bolted rabbits have a multitude of alternative warrens to head for, plus the changeable, often difficult weather conditions one has to contend with, and things tend to balance out in quite a sporting way.

When flying in hill country, one most appreciates the Harris' hawk's almost doglike attachment to its human partner. This bird really can be hunted with under the most demanding conditions. Nevertheless, it doesn't pay to take too much for granted. Contrary to popular belief, Harris' can be lost, and if a bird is to be flown in hill country, it should be gradually introduced.

Not long ago a guest came out for a day's hawking with a male Harris' which had previously been flown in rather enclosed, low-lying country. As the day progressed, he and his hawk became more and more adventurous. Although I tactfully advised him to take care, he seemed intent on casting, as it were, caution to the wind. I feel his hawk might have been a little high in weight—it was certainly very high in terms of altitude when we eventually lost sight of it.

My guest was convinced his bird had gone up onto the flat-topped grouse moor which lay above us. His casual attitude now gone, he set off in search at a brisk pace. I stuck to the lower ground and eventually located the errant Harris' down on the bottom ground where the land leveled out onto grazing fields. He looked none the worse for wear, which is more than I can say for his owner. After his expedition across the moor, my guest looked shattered.

A type of rabbit hawking with Harris' I have not seriously pursued is that of flying the bird at night with the aid of a lamp. I know one or two people who are really hooked on this nocturnal activity, but it has never really held much appeal for me. Of course, in Britain 'lamping' is normally associated with the running dog and the shooting enthusiast, and has only quite recently been employed by falconers. The main point of lamping, whether with dog, gun, or hawk, is that one can locate and approach rabbits as they feed far from cover. My main objection to lamping with hawks is that one cannot really relish being out in the countryside—or indeed the actual flights themselves—when sneaking about in the darkness.

3 The Ferruginous Hawk

Unlike the red-tailed hawk and the Harris' hawk, the ferruginous hawk, *Buteo regalis,* has not been a tremendous success in the U.K. And, compared with the two better known New World species, *regalis* has a pretty poor track record. This may be due to the fact that *regalis* is the most specialized raptor ever to be flown by hunters of ground quarries in Britain. Ignorance of this *Buteo's* specialized nature frequently leads to it being handled as if it were a red-tail. This is where the problems start, for compared to the versatile and adaptable red-tail, the ferruginous has very exact requirements in terms of hunting terrain and quarries.

The ferruginous has a very restricted natural range. By looking at this and the types of landscapes it inhabits, one begins to understand this fine *Buteo* a little better. Unlike the widespread red-tail, *regalis* is confined solely to the vast plains and deserts of western North America (its range extends just beyond the borders of the U.S.A.). Here it lives all year round and, as a species, it is classed as nonmigratory. In addition, and again unlike the red-tail, the ferruginous has no subspecies, although three color phases are recognized. These are the light phase, dark phase, and red phase. Of these, the light phase will be the one most British falconers are familiar with.

The ferruginous differs physically from the red-tail in a number of ways. First, it is a larger bird, although this is not always obvious; the ferruginous is actually heavier than it looks. Its legs are completely feathered and its feet tend to be quite small; the toes are thick and strong but the actual span of the foot is not great. A striking feature is this species' large beak area or gape. Morland Nelson feels this might help with cooling as ferruginous can be found on "south facing black cliffs," where daytime temperatures can be extremely high. Less obvious (while the bird is at rest) is that *regalis* has a narrower wing than the red-tail. In flight, the two birds are very different.

Hawking with the Ferruginous

The quarry to which the ferruginous has most frequently been flown in Britain is the rabbit. However, although in certain settings *regalis* will take rabbits, this bird is, due to the type of landscapes it requires for successful hunting, not well suited to the more typical type of rabbit hawking. This species is totally incompatible with even partially wooded areas and, if flown in any kind of enclosed country, the risk of loss is high. Also, *regalis* is most reluctant to land in trees, much preferring to use the ground. In enclosed country this can lead to all kinds of problems.

The ferruginous is far better utilized for hare hawking and once the falconer starts to think along these lines he will be working with rather than against the bird's natural instincts. Flown in wide-open country to fast, exposed quarries, a female ferruginous really comes into her own. Indeed, it is only under such conditions that one can truly appreciate this raptor. Because the ferruginous is more compatible with hares than rabbits, males of this species would need to have a question mark put over them.

Hares are very much a natural quarry for *regalis*, and in the wild this species regularly preys on black-tailed jackrabbits, *Lepus californicus*. Admittedly, it also preys heavily on much smaller animals such as ground squirrels, but the fact remains that this *Buteo* is more capable of tackling large quarry than some falconers are willing to believe.

American falconers, recognizing the natural affinity between ferruginous hawks and hares, have enjoyed more success with them than have their U.K. counterparts. In the U.S.A., both the black-tailed jackrabbit and the larger white-tailed jackrabbit, *Lepus townsendi*, have regularly been brought to bag by experienced falconers. One correspondent from Utah told me how he flew his ferruginous from the back of a pickup. With his wife in the driving seat, they would tear through the sagebrush. Apparently the truck not only acted as a mobile platform from which to hawk, but also proved to be better at flushing jackrabbits than two dozen beaters. But more importantly, it saved my correspondent from certain exhaustion. As he put it, "When you get to be fat and forty like I am, you tend to be less physical."

Of the North American hares, the white-tailed jack or prairie hare is the one which most closely resembles the European brown hare in terms of weight. Strangely enough, Frank Beebe tells me that in Ontario, where brown hares have been introduced, ferruginous are proving very successful against them. Quite interesting, really: a nonnative hawk (*regalis* does not naturally occur in Ontario) being used to hunt a nonnative hare.

For any medium-sized bird to be successful at large

hares, certain things are required. Physical fitness is important and sharp talons a must, but perhaps even more vital is the right mental attitude; the bird must be totally committed. When working with young *Buteos,* I think it very important to get them orientated to 'fur' as soon as possible. To this end, as soon as the bird is coming reliably to the fist, I immediately switch to lure work and start calling the pupil to whole dead animals of the type I eventually intend to hunt. The importance of the head hold is emphasized by allowing the bird to feed only from the head and neck area (where an incision has been made). During this period, the bird must also be taught to expect the unexpected, because wild quarry fleeing for its very life will rarely behave as predictably as the tyro might wish. With lure work, then, a little imagination is required. The lure can be made to suddenly 'appear' from various bits of undergrowth. It can be pulled in something other than a straight line, and its speed and movement can be varied. In short, it should be made to appear something like real quarry, rather than the lifeless lump it is. It is vitally important that the bird should never be allowed to take hold of a motionless lure or land nearby and hop the last foot or so. If the bird lands near to the lure, the lure must be pulled away before the bird gets to grips with it.

With young ferruginous hawks, the right kind of preparation is absolutely essential. What a pity that so many are acquired by inexperienced falconers who imagine their charges will instinctively hunt all things furred. Chase they might, in a half-hearted way, but unless the bird in question recognizes the fleeing animal as food, there will be no real commitment. And when, after each abortive attempt at quarry, the bird is recalled to some tasty tidbit on the fist, the would-be hunter is stacking the odds ever higher against himself ever achieving success.

My last ferruginous, a small female, was a typical example of a poorly trained bird. She came to me as a youngster after her original owner had decided she would never hunt. A nicer bird you would not have wished for. She was bold and steady, in perfect feather, and possessed, for a ferruginous, decently sized feet. The only problem was, she hadn't got a clue what rabbits or hares were for.

Although the season was well under way, and she should have been out in the field pursuing inexperienced quarry, I realized that I would have to go back to basics. With an ample supply of dead rabbits, I spent about ten days at home just getting her to accept these as a source of food. At first, progress was very slow, but things eventually started to come together. Then, when she was keen to feed from rabbits at home, I took her out and repeatedly flew her to a rabbit carcass in open country. Following this, and to overcome any reluctance she might show to tackle large quarry (hares), I made up a big lure out of a fox skin and got her coming to this. Not long after that, she took her first hare, and so keen was she to hunt that a week later, after being slipped at some unseen quarry, she hit a fox, which, luckily, she failed to hang on to. This was the bird that a few weeks previously had been frightened of my ferrets!

As hunting hawks in the field, the most striking thing about ferruginous hawks is their willingness and ability to take on quarry at extremely long range. Once they have notched up one or two kills, their determination has to be witnessed to be appreciated. In the right type of country, this can be put to good use, but the terrain must be very open indeed. Large, spacious fields located in an otherwise uneven landscape dotted with patches of woodland and dissected by hedgerows might appear quite suitable, but they are not. All would be well if one could guarantee the termination of a flight, successful or otherwise, within the confines of the original field, but this is simply not possible. The ferruginous that gets up to have another go at a hare it missed on the initial slip will make what seemed like open ground look all too enclosed. It is under such conditions that a ferruginous (even a big, conspicuous light phase) can be quite easily lost. Of course, the modern falconer has telemetry to assist him. While this might reduce the risk of permanent loss, it does not make enclosed country suitable to fly in nor does it make hawking in such country a rewarding experience.

Continually providing a ferruginous with ideal landscape and quarry combinations can be something of a problem for the average European falconer, and compromises will frequently have to be made. In the past, I have had some nice flights across old Second World War airfields. These places have a unique atmosphere, and one of the aerodromes I used to use was, with its control tower and buildings largely intact, quite an eerie place to be on a gray midwinter's afternoon.

I visited this old flying field a couple of seasons ago (taking a ferruginous along) and found it much changed. Farming had become quite intensive on the airfield itself, and hares were very scarce. I only saw two all morning. The first got up a long way off but the second, flushed from a strip of rough vegetation along the edge of the runway, was taken by the bird. It was an interesting flight in that I hardly saw anything of it! Round straw bales had been stacked up high along the runway, and as the hare flushed, it swung right, going through a gap in these giant bales. There was a slight oncoming breeze, and I remember thinking that if the hare had gone off in a straight line, it might have beaten the hawk into the wind. By swinging right, it had made a fatal mistake. The hawk quickly gained height, cleared the bales, and disappeared from my sight. The land which now lay ahead of the hawk was totally unrestricted and, although I saw no more of the flight, the screaming of her victim soon signaled success.

In suitable country, the ferruginous soars well and is by nature highly aerial. This species will even try to gain altitude in relatively flat fields if there is any wind. On a couple of occasions, I have had a ferruginous hit brown hares still lying in their forms from what can only be described as a low-altitude searching soar. The form made by a brown hare is little more than a depression or hollow in the earth, but it can make the occupant very difficult, or even impossible, for the falconer to spot. To the airborne hawk, the hare is obviously less invisible.

Here, a word of warning, in undulating country, it is inadvisable to give this species too much freedom when the wind is blowing. Its desire to find quarry (once entered and hunting) coupled with the effortless way in which it covers ground, can result in some tense moments. Even when flying over 'safe' soaring terrain (a lone hillside with flat country above and below), hawking with this wide-ranging species needs to be a far more controlled affair than with the Harris'.

In North America, the ferruginous has been hunted both from the fist and from a soaring position, and opinions seem to vary as to which works more effectively. A falconer from Idaho writing to me in 1984 had very clear thoughts on the subject: "If I were to fly another ferruginous, a passage would be my first choice. The eyases take a long time to develop. If I got an eyas I would want to tame hack it if at all possible. And most importantly I would fly it entirely soaring or slope soaring—the most natural way for *regalis* to hunt and the most enjoyable to watch. I flew my eyas slope soaring and she would stay on the wing for half an hour, cranking out and stooping vertically at the jackrabbits my dog would flush on the sage flats below."

Returning to European hares, although a female ferruginous is capable of taking brown hares, I feel the Scottish blue hare is a more suitable quarry. The smaller size of this upland animal and the wild open country where it is found (woodland hares excepted) suits *regalis* very well indeed.

If rabbits are to be hunted, then by far the best setting is hill country. Rabbits can sometimes be taken on low-lying agricultural ground when ferreted from isolated warrens, but for this type of hawking the ferruginous compares very poorly indeed with the goshawk and Harris' hawk.

Feathered quarries cannot be considered a serious option. Wild ferruginous do take birds, including pheasants, sage grouse, and partridge, but one must remember the type of terrain *regalis* naturally inhabits and the kind of hunting this allows. In *Hawks, Falcons and Falconry,* Frank Beebe describes the hunting tactics employed by wild ferruginous in some detail. Talking about various game birds, he says, "It is when seen in direct aerial pursuit of one of these that the speed and determination of this big hawk is most impressive. At such times they fly almost like a falcon on swept wings, with deep, strong, regular wing beats, holding a position some ten to thirteen feet behind their quarry, neither losing ground or gaining, but pacing it exactly. It follows until the quarry makes a desperate try to get down into ground cover. The instant the quarry touches the ground, the hawk accelerates and strikes." He goes on to mention that ferruginous also take much smaller birds such as meadow larks and horned larks, and then continues:

> When perched, they pay sharp attention to the flight course of all other birds seen flying. If the marked bird continues flying until it passes over the horizon, or disappears over the crest of a hill, no attempt is made to follow. But should it alight within sight, the hawk shows great interest, standing tall with head held high, marking the spot and the distance with remarkable accuracy. It then launches into swift, ground-level flight. The flight path may be direct or somewhat indirect, depending on the nature and contours of the intervening land; but the approach is always made with the last seen position of the quarry kept in mind, keeping the quarry screened behind a ridge or low obstacle. Beyond this point, the hawk seems to depend on its excellent vision and quick reflexes to discern, veer, and strike in a split-second sequence, even though the quarry may be by this time 10 to 30 feet (3 to 10 meters) from where it was originally marked. Probably most of the long aerial chases to hares or game birds are only the result of an attack of this kind being missed on the first attempt.

I can well imagine that, under the right conditions, a trained ferruginous could take feathered game on a fairly regular basis, perhaps from the soar or in a situation where the *Buteo's* persistence and staying power would be fully exploited; surely the best setting for such flights would be the country over which the bird normally hunts. Under European falconry conditions, any feathered quarries ending up in the game bag will, for the most part, be as a result of lucky encounters.

The ferruginous has been compared to the golden eagle by some writers and is often referred to as being very 'eagle like.' I am not very happy with the golden eagle comparison at all. As trained hunting birds in the field, the two raptors are quite different to work with; they also differ significantly in terms of build and shape. It could be argued that *regalis* has more in common with the steppe eagle, *Aquila rapax orientalis*, of eastern Europe and Asia. Both birds have relatively small feet for their size and have large mouths. Both will nest on the ground and both are heavily dependent (during the summer months) on small mammals. They also inhabit similar environments (steppe, desert, grassland). But such comparisons can lead one to the wrong conclusions and, although the eagle and buzzard do indeed have much in common, in many ways they are quite different. For example, the steppe eagle migrates. Of more importance to the falconer, however, is that whereas the eagle habitually preys on relatively small, weak animals, *regalis* does not and is a far more active and capable hunter.

As much as I admire this species, I truly believe that the vast majority of falconers would be far better off with a female red-tail. The ferruginous can be very interesting to fly, but only if its landscape and quarry requirements can be fully met; and only if the falconer accepts it for the specialist it is.

4 The Golden Eagle

The golden eagle, *Aquila chrysaetos*, is the largest raptor traditionally associated with falconry and, while not possessing the weight and dimensions of the very biggest eagles, it is, nevertheless, a sizable bird. As a species, it is holarctic—found in the New World south to Mexico, and across Europe and Asia south to North Africa and the Himalayas. Between three and five subspecies have been described and, as one would expect, individual birds can vary a good deal in size, depending on where they come from. Generally speaking, the largest golden eagles are found in central Asia, *A. c. daphanea*, and eastern Siberia, *A. c. canadensis*. Some authorities class the eastern Siberian birds as *A. c. kamchatika* and restrict *canadensis* to the New World. The smallest golden eagles are those from Korea and Japan and are the subspecies *A. c. japonica*.

Of all the birds I have flown for falconry purposes, this one remains closest to my heart. The golden eagle simply possesses an indefinable something special that sets it apart from other falconry birds. It is a quality which will be obvious to any serious falconer working with this raptor.

Although a number of golden eagles have been (and are) successfully flown in Britain, in many quarters they are considered unsuitable for falconry in the U.K. Why this should be is difficult to say, but perhaps English falconry literature is partly to blame, for it abounds with negative references to eagles and has surely conditioned many falconers to think of eagles as being troublesome second-rate performers.

On the Continent, things are different; in Germany, in particular, the eagle has been more appreciated. However, it must be stressed that although the golden eagle is more widely used and better understood in Germany than in the U.K., it is not a traditional bird of German falconry. The eagle's history in Germany can be traced back to 1937 when Fritz Loges became the first falconer to seriously hunt with one. Loges was fortunate in being able to obtain advice from eagle enthusiast Friedrich Remmler, who was living and hunting in Finland. With this help, Loges went on to fly his birds successfully to both hare and fox.

With Loges' death in 1955, utilization of golden eagles in Germany practically came to an end, and it was to be five years before these big hunting birds were once again seen in falconry circles. In 1960, Claus Fentzloff took up where his predecessor had left off, and at the same time a group of Austrian falconers also started working with eagles. From the period of renewed interest that followed, emerged a man who was to have a dramatic influence on the eagle scene. His name was Josef Hiebeler and today this unassuming Bavarian is regarded by many as Europe's leading authority on hunting with golden eagles.

I first met Hiebeler in central Germany, where I was working at a castle which was due to be opened as a falconry center. He had been called in to offer advice on where and how the various birds should be housed and flown. We hit it off immediately, and after working together for a couple of days, he invited me to spend some time at his own center, Schloss Rosenburg, located farther south. I needed little encouragement for, at the time, Rosenburg was something of a mecca for eagle devotees; conditions there were perfect for training and preparing eagles for the field. I eventually went to work for Hiebeler at Rosenburg, and we became firm friends.

So what made Rosenburg so special? There were many things, not least of which was the beautiful building itself. From its lofty valleyside position, it dominated the local landscape and really did make the perfect setting for a falconry center. The ground floor was purely utilitarian and contained, in addition to a small restaurant, storage rooms, a workshop, and a small equipment and weighing room. The first floor housed a museum and this, spreading through a number of rooms and corridors, was always popular with visitors, especially during periods of inclement weather. Naturally, the museum focused quite strongly on falconry and its history but the schloss and the surrounding area were also well represented.

The second floor was given over entirely to living space, the heart of which was the spacious kitchen-come-breakfast room. It was here each morning that members of the staff would assemble and discuss the day ahead. It was from here, too, that one had the best view of the surrounding area. From the kitchen window, the schloss walls just dropped away vertically for goodness knows how far. Below, the hillside was covered in broadleafed woodland and this sloped away steeply until it met the outskirts of the village.

Rosenburg's location made introducing young eagles to the joys of soaring very easy; with this, one also had feathered help. The center possessed a number of vultures (European black vultures and Griffon vultures) which were flown for visitors. These birds were old hands when it came to soaring, and knew exactly what constituted good and poor lift conditions. Flying young eagles in this type of company was of immeasurable benefit to them. It also tended to keep them on the wing when they might otherwise have been continually landing. Allowing a young eagle to soar is essential, for then the bird really learns how to fly and handle itself in the air. This is important even when the bird in question is to be used primarily for off-the-fist type flights.

But it was not always plain sailing with the vultures. Just occasionally one would go AWOL. I recall having to fetch a young Griffon from a village school where it had made an emergency landing. I arrived to find the poor bird under house arrest in the staff toilet. Another vulture, a huge European black, landed in our own car park and proceeded to destroy the seat of a very expensive motorcycle.

In addition to the demonstration vultures, which were tethered when not being flown, Rosenburg also had two Griffons which were at liberty nearly all of the time. One of these, an old zoo bird, could only fly when lift conditions were exceptionally good, but the other was frequently to be seen on the wing. This bird could be a bit of a nuisance at times. Once, during one of her patrol flights, she spotted me feeding a young eagle from a hare carcass. I was on a bit of raised ground not far from the schloss, and over she sailed looking for a handout. When nothing was produced, she went into her normal dancing routine with wings outstretched and head held high. In the end, to get some peace, I was forced to throw her the hare's innards.

Vultures were not the only soaring birds flown at Rosenburg. A variety of medium to large eagles were also used for flying displays, including Imperial and tawny eagles, bald eagles, and, for a short time, a Steller's sea eagle. But it was the golden eagles which reigned supreme and these were the only ones trained for hawking.

At falconry centers and similar establishments, one often finds that the actual hunting side of things takes a back seat. This was not so at Rosenburg. During the summer months, the emphasis might have been on flying displays and entertaining the public, but during the winter some very serious hawking was done. This meant that as the hawking season approached, one was not only doing flying displays two or three times a day, but also was training or retraining perhaps four eagles for hawking. Lure work was conducted on an open piece of land at the rear of the schloss and took several forms. Lures were pulled by hand, by jeep, or by motorcycle (more about this shortly) and, I recall, we even used a horse. With a good number of people involved, these training sessions were always enjoyable; and under Hiebeler's watchful eye, this team approach always ensured the right results. Today Josef Hiebeler runs a falconry center at a castle in Austria.

Some Considerations

The following section is not intended to be a guide to training golden eagles. Its purpose is to simply highlight one or two problem areas and look at a few points that deserve consideration. I have tried to include information that the falconer with a background of experience with other species, but no direct eagle experience, might find useful—in short, I suppose I am offering what I hope will be seen as a few helpful hints.

The first thing that needs to be addressed is the choice

between male and female eagles. When dealing with more commonly flown birds, it is more often than not simply a case of "horses of courses" with the falconer needing to look at available quarry in order to recognize which sex would better suit his or her needs. With golden eagles, the situation is somewhat different, and the vast majority of falconers really should have no decision to make. From a practical falconry point of view, the male eagle should simply be considered more desirable. I do not wish to imply females are totally unsuitable, for this they are not; indeed, in the right hands, they are capable of an awe-inspiring field performance. On the whole, however, I do feel that they are best reserved for the truly experienced specialist wishing to concentrate on the larger quarries.

In addition to the bird's sex, one will need to consider its background or origin. As license to take golden eagles from the wild in Europe are very rarely (if ever) granted, falconers are largely dependent on birds bred in captivity; and this raises the question of rearing. There are those, quite accomplished in their own particular branch of the sport who would be most reluctant to work with a golden eagle unless it had been parent reared or largely parent reared. Yet this eagle, especially if coming from a seclusion-type aviary, is without doubt inferior to one which has been carefully and professionally hand reared in the right type of stimulating and active setting.

The secret with hand-reared birds is to let the rearing process flow into training and then hunting. Once flying, they should not be subjected to lengthy periods of inactivity and should always be kept where there is plenty going on around them. Things to avoid are erratic weight control, inactivity, and solitude. Openly robbing the bird of food on the fist, or of quarry or lures, is naturally taboo.

44

Moving on to training, when flying young hand-reared eagles to the fist, certain things should be borne in mind. First, for early training sessions, a decent glove of a good length is recommended. Once the bird has been on the wing for a while and has gained experience in how to fly and, more importantly, land, a heavy glove is not so important. Second, as mentioned, the bird should never be openly robbed on the fist. This will eventually lead to it snatching at the right hand as the falconer tries to secure the jesses. It is far better to call the eagle to small tidbits on the fist and allow it to eat these without interference; the reader might be surprised just how far a young eagle will come for, say, the leg off a day-old cockerel. If the bird is a very long way off and seems reluctant to come, then, in addition to a tidbit on the fist, a slightly larger reward can be shown; but once the eagle is on the wing, this should be discreetly concealed and placed in the hawking bag. The eagle then lands and eats its tidbit as normal. If this must be done, then the additional piece of food must be put away long before the eagle comes in to land—if done without sensitivity, the bird will feel as if it has been robbed.

Staying with this subject for a moment, during training, it is a good idea to get the eagle used to being signaled with the right hand as well as being shown the garnished left fist. A circular motion works well and can be seen from a considerable distance. When a young eagle flies in and lands on the fist, its jesses must be secured. If this is not done, there is a risk the bird will grab the falconer's upper arm.

One of the largest problems facing any falconer attempting to hunt with an eagle off the fist is getting the bird fit enough to perform adequately against quarry. This is an area where techniques designed for other raptors need to be modified. In the wild, golden eagles do most of their hunting from high aloft. Accelerating away from a stand-still, in pursuit of game, is very unnatural for them. If the eagle has been flown daily under a variety of conditions, it may appear to be in form, yet this is not enough. The true hunting eagle that is required to take on long coursing-type flights demands special handling. If it is to be successful, it needs to be brought to a pitch of almost 'super fitness.'

The best way of muscling up an eagle is to have it pursue a lure that is being dragged across country by either a motorcycle or a jeep. Although all aspects of basic training are easier if one has assistance, for motorized lure work help is absolutely essential. An outline of the procedure with a motorcycle is as follows: the falconer waits with the hooded eagle (hooding should be considered mandatory) until his two assistants are in position and ready. At a sign from the falconer, they pull away, dragging the lure on a long line behind them. The eagle is unhooded and slipped. It is now vitally important that the pillion rider, holding the line, controls and times the flight perfectly. He or she must instruct the rider to either slow down or speed up, depend-ing on the eagle's distance from the lure. The raptor's inter-est must be held if a long, fast flight is to be obtained. Once it is felt that the feathered athlete has worked hard enough, he is allowed to take the lure. To avoid accidents, the line should be dropped immediately. Now the rider returns to pick up the falconer, who will be some considerable way off, while the pillion rider waits by the eagle. After the bird has been rewarded and given a short rest, the procedure is repeated in the opposite direction. As can be seen, each member of the team plays an integral role; the lure man, however, has by far the most difficult job. Riding rapidly over rough ground, looking backward in order to judge the flight and at the same time needing to instruct the rider takes skill! This type of training is highly demanding and requires a great deal of experience to operate with success; but if used carefully, it can bring golden eagles to a hard hunting pitch that few would believe possible.

Here it is perhaps worth making a few comments on lure work in general. Once a young eagle is coming well to a fox carcass or lure and is totally orientated to the head, a simulated struggle should gradually be incorporated into the daily training program. This is to be increased by degrees until quite severe. The whole point of this is to prepare the inexperienced bird for a struggle with real quarry. This type of lure work also has another important function. Young hand-reared eagles will, if allowed, become very possessive over a carcass or lure. If the bird is simply called to the lure and permitted to feed, any attempt by the falconer to make in may be resented. Yet, on the other hand, if the eagle is put through a vigorous mock battle with quarry, then its attention will be on 'killing' and holding its victim. When the falconer does approach, he will be almost ignored.

An aspect of field preparation that is often overlooked is 'woodland work.' Although golden eagles are normally flown over spacious landscapes, during training it is well worth spending some time in open woodland. This is not the easiest of places to get eagles to fly, but if introduced at an early age, they can show breathtaking ability in this environment. Woodland training helps a young eagle develop maneuverability, and it is going to need this when it comes to the business of catching quarry.

Hawking with Golden Eagles

Historically, the golden eagle is a bird of central Asian falconry. It was utilized by primarily nomadic peoples and flown to a variety of quarries, the most formidable of these being the wolf. For wolf hawking, only large female eagles were used, and these were young first-year birds trapped before they had acquired very much experience with normal prey animals. These were by far the easiest to orientate to this unnatural quarry. Training could be a pretty brutal affair, with the bird deprived of sleep for long periods by use of a swinging pole perch. It was always hooded when not being worked with, and its weight was often reduced to the point where it could no longer fly. Early lure work would simply involve the eagle pursuing on foot—half running, half flying. As it began to respond in the desired manner, its weight was slowly increased and it was then flown to a wolf lure, which would be dragged behind a horse. Hawking was done from horseback, the eagle either sitting on a T-perch (supported by the saddle) or the falconer's arm, which rested on a support. But wolf hawking was not without risk, even for the largest eagle. The late Dr. Suschkin apparently came across a trained eagle which had lost a foot while wolf hawking. Other writers even refer to birds being killed.

Hawking wolves is one aspect of eagle falconry that has remained east of the Caspian Sea and very few westerners have attempted this flight.

One exception was F. W. Remmler, who did experiment in this direction and achieved success. Wolf hawking was not Remmler's only interest. His eagles took a good many foxes and his birds were frequently flown from the saddle. He also used a T-perch; one type designed for use with a horse, another for when hawking on foot.

Beebe writes that coyotes are not considered a hazardous quarry for female golden eagles. I am not sure how many U.S. falconers have actually put this to the test, but I would imagine that coyote hawking over desert or prairie landscapes would closely emulate the Asian wolf experience, especially if conducted from horseback.

On a similar theme, in 1974 Claus Fentzloff and Jacques Renaud were invited to Morocco for what was to be a very different type of hawking experience. Flying three golden eagles over extremely harsh terrain, they accounted for no less than six jackals.

Foxes

While this quarry is considered well suited to the golden eagle, flights to fox should not be viewed in a matter-of-fact manner. Not that the quarry is too much for an eagle; any bird that can hold a full-grown wolf can certainly deal with a red fox. In fact, Reynard is well within the capabilities of an average male eagle; but for the bird to be truly effective against the fox, it must be correctly prepared. The young eagle that has been incorrectly trained with small lures will not usually demonstrate much enthusiasm for tackling a large, and very much alive, fox. That said, totally inexperienced eagles do sometimes take (or attempt to take) the first fox they see. Yet, when this happens, there is normally some explanation. Often the quarry will have been only partially seen due to some crop or other cover, and the bird takes it before realizing its true identity. The serious falconer will leave less to chance and do the groundwork thoroughly.

Of all the different peoples that have hunted fox (and wolf) with eagles, the Kirghiz and Kazakhs are surely the best known. There can be few eagle devotees that have not, at one time or another, imagined what it would be like to hunt in the eagle's true homeland alongside these falconers. Although, today, far better eagle falconry is seen in the

West, central Asia is still alluring to those interested in golden eagles, in the same way as Arabia is to those fascinated by falcons. In 1990, Josef Hiebeler and two other German friends were lucky enough to spend some time in Kazakhstan hawking with native falconers. The trip was something of an expedition, and the setting was very remote, so remote in fact that for the last leg of the journey the party was flown in by helicopter. They took no birds with them, but relied on eagles provided by their hosts. Hawking was conducted from horseback, and this required some getting used to. All of the party could ride, but none had done any serious hunting from the saddle. In addition, the birds were being carried right-handed, as is the tradition in Asia. But these things were soon adjusted to. The eagles themselves were passage birds and kept in extremely sharp hunting form. It was also noted that none of them were capable of taking on any kind of strenuous coursing-type flights. But this seemed to matter little, as they were being flown primarily across ridges and hills (in direct pursuit—not soaring). When not being flown, the birds spent most of their time hooded. From a practical falconry point of view, the trip was not a great success, and although several foxes were caught, quarry was quite scarce. Nevertheless, hawking pure and simple had not been the main reason for going, and, all in all, the trip was deemed extremely worthwhile.

Feral Cats
A casual glance might lead the uninitiated observer to believe that a feral cat would be easily dealt with by an eagle. But looks, as they say, can be deceiving, and, as a quarry, the feral cat demands a great deal of respect, if not so much from the sporting angle then because of its lethal nature.

Flights to cats, and let me assure the reader I am talking about truly feral animals, can be hazardous. The cat is tough, strong, and extremely well armed—and will fight it out 'tooth and nail' if given the chance. I do not wish to make this quarry out to be some kind of tiger, for that it is not—in fact, it gets taken by smaller raptors than golden eagles; but considering the amount of sport there is to be had, it hardly seems worth risking injury to a valuable bird. Some falconers will fly at them; many more, however, prefer not to.

Roe Deer

Like the fox and wolf, 'hoofed' animals such as gazelle, deer, and saiga antelope have been a quarry for golden eagles for centuries. This type of hawking remained something of a mystery until central Asia became more accessible to westerners, then slowly, accounts of deer hawking filtered back to Europe. The writings of several early travelers mention eagles being used to hunt all manner of large quarry, including deer. One also finds evidence of these flights in the reports of Marco Polo. Many of these early and often 'colorful' accounts were taken none too seriously, and apparently even T. W. Atkinson, writing as late as 1860, was to have his description viewed with a degree of skepticism. This is what he had to say:

> We had not gone far when several large deer rushed past a jutting point of the reeds and bounded over the plain, about 300 yards from us. In an instant the Bearcoote was unhooded and his shackles removed, when he sprang from his perch, and soared up into the air. I watched him ascend as he wheeled round, and was under the impression that he had not seen the animals; but in this I was mistaken. He had now risen to a considerable height

and seemed to poise himself for about a minute. After this he gave two or three flaps of his wings and swooped off in a straight line toward his prey. I could not perceive that his wings moved, but he went at a fearful speed. There was a shout and away went his keepers at full gallop, followed by many others.

I gave my horse his head and a touch of the whip; in a few minutes he carried me to the front, and I was riding neck and neck with one of the keepers. When we were about 200 yards off the Bearcoote struck its prey. The deer gave a bound forward, and fell. The Bearcoote had struck one talon into his neck and the other into his back, and with his beak was tearing out the animal's liver.

The Kirghis sprang from his horse, slipped the hood over the eagle's head and shackles upon his legs, and removed him from his prey without difficulty. The keeper mounted his horse, his assistant placed the Bearcoote on his perch, and he was ready for another flight. No dogs are taken out when hunting with the eagle, they would be destroyed for a certainty; indeed the Kirghis assert that he will attack and kill the wolf.

It is all to easy for the modern falconer to criticize aspects of Atkinson's story, but let us allow him a little artistic license. The fact that he witnessed deer being taken with eagles is beyond doubt.

Deer hawking is something for the skilled specialist working with a carefully prepared bird, and it is here that the female eagle really does have something to offer. Not that acquiring a female eagle is an answer in itself; nothing could be further from the truth, for although any healthy female possesses the physical power to take roe deer, convincing her of the fact can prove a problem.

As with fox, an occasional deer might be taken by an average female or even male eagle (some males make excellent deer eagles) if the conditions are right. A roe deer running through cover or perhaps in some brushy hollow, exposing only its upper body, might prove irresistible to any sharp eagle. Such chance encounters do occur and can result in roe being taken. However, bringing an eagle to a pitch where it will hunt deer in a predictable manner in the open, with no cover to disguise the quarry's size, is something not to be taken lightly. The bird will require a very individual type of schooling.

Although in Britain the roe deer is an animal associated primarily with woodland and forest, in other parts of Europe it is often found in very open terrain indeed. One immediately thinks of Hungary and the former Czechoslovakia, but in parts of Austria, too, one can encounter roe in quite exposed locations. On open, cultivated land, there is normally the odd rough patch, perhaps part of an old overgrown ditch or a bit of ground that has not, or for some reason cannot, be worked. It is here that one stands a chance of putting up roe deer. Actually, it really is quite amazing just how well concealed an adult roe can remain even in very sparse cover. In eastern Europe, one can have them materialize, from nowhere, in flat, treeless country. It is in such settings that one sees this beautiful deer at her best, and it is here that roe hawking is most spectacular.

Spectacular is a word that definitely describes a roe flight I witnessed a couple of seasons ago. But no flat land flight this and certainly no typical or normal flight in any sense. A days hawking had been arranged in some very hilly country, the type of country where if you are not climbing up, you are scrambling down. On reaching the top of a ridge, a group of roe deer were spotted. They were far below and some way off. No one really considered it a viable hawking opportunity but an experienced deer eagle (a male belonging to J. Hiebeler) was unhooded and allowed to fly. The eagle left the hillside in the general direction of the deer, which were now heading for an area of woodland. Strangely, the eagle made no effort to close with any of the deer but actually gained height. Then, with the deer just entering the woods, he folded up and went into an almost vertical stoop. The deer had now disappeared among the trees and everyone fully expected the eagle to pull out of his stoop. But this he did not. Instead, he went in through the trees and was lost from sight. Helter-skelter down the hill went the hawking party, hurrying but not really expecting the bird to have been successful; but here again a surprise was in store. After a long search, the eagle was located attached firmly to one very dead female roe deer. Piecing together what had taken place was not difficult. The ground had been disturbed over some distance and on being inspected, the deer was found to have a huge deep gash on one flank; this obviously made by the eagle as it hit her traveling too fast to hang on. The wound, as frightful as it was, had not killed the deer immediately (evidence on the disturbed woodland floor supported this). From the point of impact she had continued to run or stagger a little way until the eagle had bounced off the ground and bound firmly to her head. The flight was unusual in two respects, one being the terrain and mode of attack. The other being the fact that the deer had been killed outright by the eagle. This happens very infrequently and normally the falconer needs to dispatch the quarry.

When hunting roe deer, one glimpses a side of the golden eagle not seen by those who employ the bird solely for hunting smaller quarry. It has nothing to do with flight style or the quality of flights; it is simply the birds ability to deal so effectively with such a large animal. The eagle's raw power is, of course, immediately exposed but it is the bird's guts and determination which really impress. One sees the golden eagle's very special mentality fully unveiled, and it is this mentality combined with its physical attributes that makes the finely tuned hunting eagle so devastating.

Brown Hares

The brown hare is the quarry most frequently taken with golden eagles in Europe; although several medium-sized raptors will, if exactingly trained, also account for hares, the eagle's performance will be difficult to match. Indeed, for intensive hawking in hare-rich country, a male golden eagle can safely be considered the ultimate hare-hawk.

Having said that, it must be added that golden eagles require a lot of work before they start to shine in flights to hares; young eagles (especially females) normally find all but the easiest hares difficult. It is not so much the physical business of subduing the quarry (although young male eagles do occasionally get kicked off hares) as it is the actual catching of it. The brown hare's phenomenal speed is legendary and it is this speed, coupled with the ability to jink, jump, and even stop dead in a fraction of a second, that often leaves the inexperienced eagle bewildered and bemused.

Assuming that the eagle is being flown by a skilled falconer, the amount of success experienced is going to depend largely on exposure to quarry. Unless the bird can be shown a large number of hares, progress will be slow. Not that the bird should be slipped at each and every hare, no matter where it gets up; such a course of action would be disastrous. But unless one has an abundance of hares, the right number of suitable slips cannot be guaranteed. It really does pay to pick slips carefully, and here terrain can play an important role. Smooth and even fields might look very tempting, but on such surfaces a hare is in her element; far better to look for hares on ground where they will be hindered in some way—for example, on really deep, rough plow; and the deeper the furrows and the more uninviting it looks to walk over the better. On this type of terrain the hare's maneuverability is greatly reduced and even the most inexperienced bird will be in with a chance.

Shorter slips will generally be had when there is some form of ground cover. Hares frequently shelter in root crops during the day and some interesting flights are to be had here. Late in the season, short winter wheat can provide some ideal slips, as can an area of canola. When hawking any really prime spot, care must be taken not to 'waste' hares. If the bird misses a hare, try to get it back to the fist with as little fuss as possible. Altering position and meandering about might well result in another hare being flushed with the bird impossibly placed to even attempt it.

Many experienced falconers fly their eagles 'out of the hood.' This can work very well indeed, especially with birds that are prone to be a bit restless when carried bare headed. A bird that is constantly bating can be very tiresome to carry, but, more importantly, it is wasting its own energy. The hooded bird remains calm and composed and is ready to give its best when a suitable hawking opportunity presents itself. Falconers who do not hood their eagles often claim that valuable time is lost by flying out of the hood and that the unhooded bird reacts much faster. This is not a truly valid argument against hooding, as the amount of quarry taken by birds flown out of the hood testifies. If the eagle has been carefully made to the hood and has been conditioned to be flown out of the hood throughout its training period, then very little time is lost when it comes to slipping at quarry. The hood is quickly removed and the bird expects to see game. There is no hesitation; the bird is on the wing in an instant. For this type of flying, Kirghiz and Kazakh hoods work well as they have no braces. If Anglo-Indian (or similar) pattern hoods are being used, then the braces are closed just enough to keep the hood on but not enough to prevent its instant removal. Flying out of the hood at hares has just one disadvantage. The hooded bird cannot spot squatting hares lying in their forms, and often it is the eagle's behavior that tells the falconer he is right on top of a hare.

Squatting hares might seem a very easy option, but it doesn't pay to rush things—a little care is required. If a hare is spotted, the falconer should back off and, if possible, get someone else to flush it. If the eagle is hooded (the falconer having spotted the hare), then the hood should be removed before the hare is flushed. It is also wise to note which way the hare is facing so that a suitable position for the slip can be taken up. Hares are frequently missed when they are simply kicked up from underfoot and the eagle overflies them as they put in a first quick jink.

Depending on the time of year and how the land is being farmed, on agricultural ground one can often spot hare forms from quite a distance. The small amount of soil pushed up out of a form can look quite conspicuous on an otherwise flat, even expanse. One may come across several empty forms; if nothing else, these indicate the likely presence of a hare or hares, and by the time an occupied form is located (or a hare put up) you are bound to be on your toes.

Although irregular 'lumps' and 'bumps' are well worth investigating, more often than not there will be no visual evidence of hares until one is up and running. A hare can blend into the barest of fields, and because of this one can never relax. A casual approach will result in borderline slips being missed, or hares being walked over when they are sitting tight.

In flat, open country, the wind can be a bit of a problem, and on really windy days, there are only two practical ways to conduct business; one either hunts with or across the wind. Even a super fit eagle slipped into a strong wind will be at a terrific disadvantage and has little hope of connecting with quarry. However, if downwind flights can be organized, then the scene is set for some very fast action. With the wind behind those seven-foot sails, an eagle can really cover country, the only snag being the bird's reduced control. More wind equals more speed but less maneuverability. So if the stubble is being ripped out by its roots, then working across wind might be more advisable.

Wind in hill country is a different thing altogether, and some fine soaring is to be had with golden eagles. Some years ago I knew a falconer who was flying his eagle (a female) in no other way than from the soar. He simply would not fly the bird off the fist in flat country. The type of hawking experienced by this chap was quite spectacular, and in the high, lonely country he hawked over, some very dramatic flights were seen. But the flights were not only dramatic, they were also very productive. As the seasons went by, this eagle became a truly efficient hunter. Her main quarry was rabbits, but she also took hares. It was interesting that on the way to the hawking land, her owner would always keep a lookout for hang gliders. Depending on how and where these were flying, he reckoned he could judge how the lift conditions would be on his patch.

On arriving at the farm, he would remove the eagle from his old battered van and carry her, hooded, up the hillside. Once far enough up the hill, she was unhooded and allowed to fly in her own time. Off she would go, using the lift and then come back overhead waiting to be served. Her pitch would, of course, vary depending on wind conditions. On a good day she might go very high indeed. Just how high is difficult to say, and falconers can all too easily overestimate the height of their birds—be they falcons or eagles. This particular chap always seemed pretty conservative with his estimates, and confessed that he was no great judge of height, but one can safely say that a pitch of 1,000 feet or more was not unusual for this bird.

Once quarry was spotted, the eagle's attack varied depending on her position in relation to the fleeing animal. Most spectacular were the vertical stoops with the bird completely folded up and literally plummeting to earth. This breathtaking sight is what her owner loved to see more than anything—and is it any wonder?

I am often asked to describe a 'typical' hare flight with a golden eagle. This is very difficult to do as, even in flat country, these flights are less predictable than one might imagine. One hare might get up quite close, run straight ahead, and be taken by the bird without ever deviating from its original line. Another might jink left or right, causing the eagle to overshoot, and then head off again in a straight line; it may spin right around and head off in the opposite direction. The eagle might be beaten by the first sharp turn, or make a number of attempts at the same hare; it might have to pick itself up off the ground in order to have another go, or it might manage to stay airborne throughout several of the hare's maneuvers.

Nice flights are seen when a hare being closely pursued stops dead, and the eagle throws up and comes straight down at it from above.

A perfect example of this kind of flight was captured on video by Terry Large quite recently. Falconers and beaters were lined up working each side of a deep, dry ditch. I was on the ditch's right-hand bank with a friend, rummaging through the undergrowth in the ditch. I felt fairly well placed for a flight or two. Left and right the countryside was flat with no cover of any description. Surely, if we were going to move anything at all it would be from the ditch—wrong. After a little while, it seemed that everyone was getting flights except for me! But on the smooth, bare ground hares were not sitting tight at all and in the main they were getting up out of range; it was to be one of these 'out of range' hares that was to provide Terry with his bit of video action.

The hawking line had become uneven; those on the left-hand side of the ditch were further back than those of us on the right. This meant that a hare getting up too far ahead in front of the left-hand group might provide a viable slip for someone on the right. So it was that I found myself presented with an irresistible opportunity. A hare was flushed some way off to the left. Had it run straight ahead, it would not have been worth considering; it was simply too far away. But it departed at an angle and its route brought it within slipping distance. I unhooded the eagle and he was away, and in that instant the hare changed course. The chase was on with eagle and hare eating up the ground in full view of the field. The eagle closed the gap and was just about to commit himself when the hare hit the brakes. The eagle threw up and just how high he went was quite surprising. Watching the play-back on Terry's video you see the hare stop and the eagle go vertically out of the picture; it stays out of the picture for so long you imagine it has either landed elsewhere or gone into orbit! Then down it comes back into the picture, dropping like a stone; the hare side-steps and takes off again—the eagle hits the dry bare ground so hard it sends a cloud of dust into the air.

The most effective anti-eagle maneuver is the vertical jump. This is put to good use on inexperienced and experienced birds alike. It all happens in a split second. Just as hare and eagle seem to merge as one, the hare catapults itself skyward and the eagle is left on the ground wondering what happened. It is such a spectacular feat that one cannot begrudge the hare her escape.

In the chapter on the ferruginous hawk, I mentioned hares being spotted in their forms by airborne hawks. One also sees this with golden eagles and some birds became quite proficient at spotting squatters from the air. On one occasion, I was heartily congratulated by several enthusiastic beaters for the long and difficult flight my eagle had successfully taken on. But they hadn't seen the flight clearly. The eagle had missed the initial 'sporting' hare (this went into a ditch I think), gained a little height, and taken one which flushed from its form right beneath him. This second hare had, in fact, run less than ten yards! I kept quiet and reveled in the praise.

I think that many falconers who fly smaller hawks to hares imagine that once an eagle and hare make contact, the result is a foregone conclusion. This is not so. Eagles certainly can lose hares, especially inexperienced birds. Sometimes a hare escapes due to an eagle being fumble footed (one sees this often with young birds that have not been taught the importance of securing a head hold). At other times, the conditions under which the hare is being flown play a part. Imagine a hare running down a bank of rock-hard, broken ground; behind it is a young male eagle traveling at speed. The two come together and cartwheel end over end. The impetus tears them apart and both end up sitting flat on the ground some distance apart.

Some interesting flights were had by Josef Hiebeler and I one year when, for a brief period, we flew a cast of male eagles at hares. It was not something we really planned, as such. Both of us were working with young birds, and we decided to try training them together rather than individually. This was at Schloss Rosenburg, where conditions were extremely favorable. The birds were flown in each other's company from early on. We allowed them to soar together and they were lure-trained together.

For serious lure work, fox and roe deer lures were pulled behind a Range Rover. For this, four people were needed, one to drive, one in the back controlling the lure line, and two people to fly the eagles. No crabbing or fighting on the lure (or lure-carcass) was experienced, but playing safe, whoever got to them first (one of us was always in the Range Rover) slipped a hawking bag between them. Naturally, they needed to be carefully introduced to this kind of thing. Initially, we simply sat with them, holding their jesses short as they fed from different areas of a carcass.

We took these eagles to a hawking meet in Austria. I think this was in late October, but I am not quite sure. What I am sure about is that we should have told the rest of the people in our group what we were up to. As both eagles took off simultaneously in pursuit of their first hare, I thought the chap next to me was going to have a heart attack. His condition was not helped as the two birds powered in for the kill, first one, then a second later, the other.

I believe we ended up catching three or four hares at the Austrian meet, one of them getting up from behind the line (after being walked over) and heading off at full speed across a bare earth field where one would have expected to spot a squatting mouse let alone a hare. I am reminded of this hare not so much because of the flight but because of the behavior of one chap's young son. The sprightly lad sped off after the eagles like a whippet. He was at the scene of the kill before anyone else and we arrived to find him carefully holding the tail feathers of one of the eagles to prevent them suffering damage on the hard ground. Apparently he had got into the habit of doing this when out with his father and goshawk. While his father dispatched and dealt with the hare, he kept the birds' tail feathers folded together and straight. On this particular day, his helpful gesture was quite unnecessary. A golden eagle's plumage can stand an awful lot of abuse and anyway, with two eagles attached to it the hare was not struggling much.

What was interesting to observe whenever these eagles flew together was just how differently they behaved in the air. This was quite obvious during training but their individual flight styles were most easily discernible when hunting. Of course, one expects golden eagles to differ from bird to bird (and not only in flying style) but when one is constantly flying two together one has an opportunity to make immediate comparisons which are not often afforded. My bird, which was the slightly smaller of the two, was definitely faster than his companion and when hunting was determined to the point of being reckless. He also possessed that lust to fly and keep flying which some young eagles have and some do not. I suppose he could have been described as hyperactive.

Josef's bird was very different. Physically it had a more squat appearance with a proportionately larger head; it also had larger feet. Compared to the one I was flying, this bird was calm and steady and far less hectic. Not exactly thrilling to watch in flight but a keen hunter, and its more controlled approach balanced out my bird's reckless 'any which way' attitude. Together they worked well.

I feel it important to add that the novice should not consider the flying of golden eagles together as the norm, or something which can simply be undertaken as is often the case with Harris' hawks, for example.

As this is the last time the subject of hare hawking will be discussed in any detail, I would like to make a few comments on slipping, or to be more specific, slipping distances. The novice may feel that I have been a little vague about just what constitutes viable or nonviable slip; the more experienced falconer will understand my reluctance to lay down exact distances. Out in the field, one encounters so many variables that a measurement of distance alone means nothing. One has to account for things such as the nature of the landscape (flat, undulating, hilly), the surface the hare is running on (smooth and 'fast' or uneven), and of course, whether the hare is running into the wind or downwind. To these considerations one has to add information about the eagle: its experience and level of fitness. Asking at what distance can an eagle take hares is not what one could term a straightforward question.

Let's move from golden eagles to goshawks for a moment. Goshawks are generally considered short-range sprint specialists, but even with these confusion can arise regarding slipping at hares. One respected German author recommends slips of twenty to forty yards while one English author talks of 100 yard slips.

The first set of figures is quite in order as a general guide. With the latter distance, one needs additional information, and this the author gives when he says that the hare will not feel under threat and therefore not run at her top speed. This highlights another factor for the novice to bear

Russian falconer with Siberian goshawk—*A. g. albidus.*

Photo: T. Dollmann

European goshawk in flight.

Head study of a German goshawk.

European goshawk.

European goshawk coming into adult plumage.

Adult North American goshawk.

Photos: C. Kellogg

Immature North American goshawk.

Adult North American goshawk.

Photos: C. Kellogg

A hunter in the making!

Rabbit hawking in the snow with a goshawk.

Photos: D. Kuhn

Opposite top: Goshawk pursuing a rabbit.
Opposite bottom: Goshawk with rabbit.

Rabbit hawking in the snow with a goshawk.

One rabbit and *two* many goshawks—a situation one should always try to avoid

Goshawk and rabbit.

when hunting with goshawks.
Goshawk and brown hare.

Photos: D. Kuhn

Goshawk and brown hare—the great escape!

Photo: D. Kuhn

German rabbit hawkers.

Photo: Author

North American goshawk on cottontail.

Photos: C. Kellogg

How not to remove a hawk from its kill!

Above: Immature North American goshawk. *Photo: C. Kellogg*
Right: Adult North American gos. *Photo: C. Kellogg*
Below: Adult Cooper's hawk with flicker at pluming perch. *Photo: R. Kline*

Eleven-year-old female red-tail belonging to Clifford Kellogg with San Juan Island, Washington, cottontail.

Photo: C. Kellogg

A Harris' hawk on the hill.

Female Harris' hawk.

Harris' hawk. *Photo: R. Kline*

Harris' hawk. *Photo: R. Kline*

A Harris' gets his reward. *Photos: C. Kellogg*

Hawking brown hares with a goshawk can be a rough business.

Photos: D. Kuhn

Tom Boulton with dark-phase female ferruginous hawk.

Female ferruginous with rabbit.

Ferruginous hawk belonging to Frank Beebe of Sidney, British Columbia.

Photos: C. Kellogg

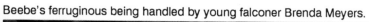

Beebe's ferruginous being handled by young falconer Brenda Meyers.

Hunting with golden eagles, Kazakhstan 1990.

Photo: T. Dollmann

Kazakhstan 1990.

Base camp—Kazakhstan.

Head study of female golden eagle.

Photo: Author

Golden eagle x steppe eagle hybrid.

Photo: T. Dollmann

Author with a male golden eagle.

Two male eagles being trained together.

Golden eagle after hare.

Two golden eagles behind a hare.

Golden eagle and hare.   *Photos: D. Kuhn*

Golden eagle and hare.

Golden eagle and hare—shot one.

Photos: D. Kuhn

Golden eagle and hare—shot two.

Golden eagle and hare—shot three.

Shot four—up, up, and away!

Accidents can happen—too many eagles!

Photo: T. Dollmann

Golden eagle and hare.
Photo: T. Dollmann

Golden eagle and hare.
Photo: D. Kuhn

Golden eagle and almost a hare—shot one.

Photos: D. Kuhn

Golden eagle saying good-bye to the hare—shot two.

Taking the lure at speed.

Photo: Author

Missing hare at same speed.

Photo: D. Kuhn

Golden eagle pursuing a roe deer.

Photo: D. Kuhn

Golden eagle with roe deer.

Photo: Author

Golden eagle with fox.   *Photo J. Hiebeler*

End of a successful fox flight—Kazakhstan.   *Photo: T. Dollmann*

Golden eagle group in Czechoslovakia.

The weathering area at Opocno, 1992.

Someone with something to smile about.

Photo: T. Dollmann

A mixed hawking group takes a break—Czechoslovakia, 1985.

Photo: Author

Ferreting equipment.

in mind; hares flushed close and put under pressure and hares spotted some way off and perhaps leaving in no great hurry.

Under the right conditions, a good golden eagle can take on hares at extremely long range, but the less experienced falconer would be advised to keep slips short and pick slips carefully (as already mentioned) until he has learned something about the bird's capabilities and something about the quarry he is pursuing. With time, one develops an almost sixth sense or gut feeling about hare flights, one simply knows when a slip is viable or not. The experienced falconer will see things his less experienced companion will not. More importantly, he will be able to assess a given situation in a split second and therefore fully exploit any opportunity that arises.

Eagles and Dogs

Golden eagles and hawking dogs are often considered a bad combination; the reason being that the dog will be at risk from the eagle. Generally speaking this is not true. If the eagle has been handled and trained correctly and introduced to dogs in a sensible manner, it will not attempt to murder its canine companion at every opportunity.

Abused eagles, or eagles which have been simply retained rather than trained, can be a different matter and with these poor creatures problems can arise. Just recently, a friend had to abandon hopes of flying an eagle he acquired as a 'hand me down' over his weimaraner bitch. The eagle (a female) would pile into the dog whenever it could—what a pity she didn't show the same sort of aggression when faced with roe deer!

I think it important to add that even when dealing with an eagle which is regularly flown over a dog, one must be careful about where one hunts. It would be extremely fool-ish to fly a sharp hunting eagle in an area where strange, unfamiliar dogs may be encountered; this would be asking for trouble.

5 Hybrids

The crossing of various raptors to produce hybrids has been going on for years. One sees it done more commonly with falcons (such as a gyr x saker cross) but *Buteo, Accipiter*, and even eagle hybrids of one type or another have occurred. For someone not involved in falconry an immediate question regarding hybrids would surely be—why? And even for many who actively practice the sport the value of, or need for, hybrid hunting birds is not always clear.

Of course, in many cases hybrids are produced simply because for some reason the 'genuine article' is not viable. It is often a case of hybrid or nothing. This is indeed frequently the case with the more recent *Buteo* x *Buteo* hybrids and golden eagle hybrids.

However, the real impetus for producing these hybrids probably comes from two totally artificial methods to bypass misdirected anticonservation wildlife laws. First, wildlife laws in many countries greatly restrict both movement of birds within and between countries. While conservation laws should encourage the captive breeding of predators (and other animals for that matter), these ill thought-out laws greatly reduce the number of birds available for falconry or release out into the wild. Second, because of these restrictive laws, many hawk breeders have literally been forced into breeding hybrids to circumvent the restrictive laws that apply to purebred species. In many thousands of years, falconry has supported the conservation of birds of prey. Nevertheless, today there certainly seems to be more interest in producing hybrid *Buteos* or eagles than was previously the case.

With deliberately produced hybrids the question of why still needs to be looked at. What could a hybrid *Buteo* offer over a pure Harris', red-tail, or ferruginous? There have been various arguments put forward and just how much sense these make depends very much on the hybrid in question. For example, I can see little point in deliberately producing Harris' x ferruginous or ferruginous x Harris' hybrids. The Harris' is such a good all rounder, why dabble. And really, the ferruginous is such a specialist that I would think twice about using it for producing any hybrid. Of course, hare and jackrabbit hawkers might feel that ferruginous blood would give a female Harris' the advantage of a bit more weight and strength. But for hare hawking pure and simple, it could just as easily be argued that a big purebred female ferruginous or better still, male golden eagle would fit the bill very nicely indeed.

Certainly one or two of my British hawk breeding friends find the thought of producing big hare catching hybrids very interesting; but more perhaps because of their novelty value than anything else. I wonder if there would be a demand from serious falconers for such hybrids in Britain. After all, it must be remembered that in Britain the hare (*L. capensis* or *L. timidus*) is not as important to falconry as the humble rabbit. In the United States hares are more seriously pursued and so perhaps U.S. falconers would be the ones to really appreciate heavyweight hybrids, be they ferruginous x Harris' or ferruginous x red-tail combinations. I can image that those falconers hawking, or attempting to hawk big burly white-tailed jackrabbits with female red-tails or female Harris' hawks would welcome something with a bit more punch.

The first choice of many Continental hare hawkers is the golden eagle, but even this species has been 'modified.' A German friend currently owns a golden eagle x steppe eagle hybrid. This bird has been flown successfully to brown hares, but a golden eagle hybrid containing steppe eagle blood is a watered down rather than beefed up version of the purebred bird. In truth, there is no other member of the genus *Aquila* that could add anything to the golden eagle's already impressive capabilities.

While I can sympathize to a degree with the interest in hybridizing *Buteos*, I feel the production of *Accipiter* hybrids or, as was recently achieved, *Accipiter* x *Parabuteo* hybrids, would be more difficult to justify. For hawking rabbits and large feathered quarries, what can really match a pure female goshawk? And for small feathered game, sparrow hawks and Cooper's hawks have never been found lacking.

I am not really for or against hybrids of any description, but for hawking ground game I feel they should be viewed (by the experienced falconer) as an interesting alternative rather than seen by the novice as some kind of magical answer to his or her falconry problems.

Falcons and 'Fur'

Although this book concerns itself primarily with goshawks, *Buteos*, and eagles, it would be wrong, especially after mentioning hybrids, not to at least acknowledge the possibility of flying falcons to ground quarry.

In Europe and North America, falcons are associated very much with feathered game, but elsewhere some falcon species have a long tradition of being used to hunt mammalian quarry.

When one thinks of flights to 'fur,' the saker falcon comes immediately to mind and is perhaps best known for its role in gazelle hunting. The saker was not required to bring down the gazelle single-handed but by repeatedly stooping at and harrying the animal it gave the saluki or salukis chance to come up on it.

Hares have long been a quarry for female sakers in Arabia and central Asia; in eastern Europe, too, sakers have occasionally been flown to hares. Adult European brown hares are a tough quarry for a saker and many would argue that one is pushing the bird to the limit of its capabilities, if not beyond. But success can be achieved in this area as falconers such as Ivan Maroši have shown. Ivan has spent a great deal of time pursuing hares in eastern Europe with a variety of raptors, including sakers.

Flights to brown hares with sakers differ quite significantly to those seen with shortwings or broadwings. Sometimes the saker will bind immediately goshawk fashion but more normally puts in several stoops first. Ivan tells me that the number of stoops is influenced by the size of the hare, the bird's experience, and her weight. If too sharp, she may go in immediately for the kill but not have the strength to deal with the hare; if too 'high,' she may refuse to bind but keep on stooping at the fleeing hare in a halfhearted way.

Female gyr falcons have shown themselves to be a match for the largest hares. Indeed, around 1860, several gyr falcons were kept at Elvden in Britain specifically for hare hawking. How much success was achieved at Elvden is not clear but the surrounding countryside was apparently well suited to the flight and hares were abundant. I feel sure that some of the big gyr x sakers being produced would be just the job for flights to hares (or jackrabbits) in very open country. One would have the weight and power of gyr with the durability and toughness of the saker.

In North America female prairie falcons have accounted for jackrabbits and in Britain, blue hares have been taken 'by accident' by grouse hawkers flying peregrines. I recall watching a gutsy little tiercel knock the wind out of a cock pheasant, throw up, and then stoop at a rabbit which had obviously been disturbed by the commotion. The rabbit recovered (as did the pheasant) but not before being rolled head over heels.

6 To and from the Field

The modern falconer has come to consider traveling with his hawks as the norm. For some, it is an almost daily routine throughout the season. Those falconers flying middleweight all-rounders such as goshawks and Harris' hawks, tend to be less reliant on the automobile, being fairly flexible regarding where and what they hunt. Nevertheless, even these people, if of the 'have hawk will travel' kind, will frequently find themselves undertaking long journeys with their charges.

When transporting a hawk, there are a number of considerations, but its safety, comfort, and well-being should be of primary importance. Whether traveling five miles or fifty, unless the bird arrives relaxed and calm, any idea of hawking can be forgotten, at least until it has had time to settle down.

Many falconers are quite happy to travel with a bird sitting on a bow perch in the back of an estate car; often the bird seems quite happy with this arrangement, too. Sometimes the back of a seat is employed as a perch—sometimes a passenger's hand. But this type of thing has obvious disadvantages, especially if one also has dogs, ferrets, company, and, perhaps, another hawk along for the trip. One also has to consider what would happen if the car broke down or there were an accident. And it is not only hunters of ground game who need to think carefully about transporting their birds. I was told about a group of grouse hawkers who, on a pilgrimage north, returned to their vehicle to find a female peregrine upside down, clinging to the car's roof lining.

The easiest and safest way of transporting goshawks, *Buteos,* and eagles is to use custom-made hawk boxes. This takes all the worry out of traveling. My own preference is for solid boxes without any form of window in them, but some Harris' owners report that their birds travel better in boxes which have a 'viewing port' build in. With goshawks, I have tended to use boxes with perches in them, but with Harris', ferruginous hawks, and eagles, I never use a perch; the bird sits flat on the floor of the box. A snugly fitting piece of carpet is placed in the bottom of the box and before each trip this is covered with newspaper. Penetrating yesterday's headlines, the bird's talons find a firm hold while precious tail tips are given some protection by the smooth newspaper. That's the idea, anyway. Often one opens the box to find the paper completely shredded.

As strange as it may sound, golden eagles can be almost box trained in much the same way as a dog or cat is house trained. On very long journeys, one simply stops every two hours and removes the eagle from its box. Individual birds actually get into the habit of waiting for this traveling break and make good use of it. A quiet spot is recommended, as such goings on attract attention. On one occasion, I was traveling back from a hawking meet with some friends when we were forced to stop at a busy motorway service station. Removing four eagles from their boxes, we stood there surrounded by inquisitive onlookers. Slowly, one by one, our charges ejected a very visual reminder of how successful the hunting had been.

I suppose I have experimented with most kinds of hawk boxes. At one time I built a rather elaborate collapsible affair for carrying a goshawk in the back of an old VW Beetle. I made it collapsible to please my girlfriend, who insisted she couldn't safely use the car with the box in one piece. She certainly had a point as, when in use, the box ensured that the bird had more room and comfort than the driver or passenger! Normally speaking, I like to keep boxes as simple as possible, but whether they are of an upright design and contain a perch, or are elongated and intended for a floor-sitting bird, they must conform in certain ways. The inside must be smooth (melamine if possible); there must be sufficient head and tail clearance; hinges and other fittings must be flush; and it must be well ventilated.

7 Field Meetings

People who join falconry clubs do so for a variety of reasons. Some simply wish to 'belong.' Others may recognize certain benefits, while the more noble at heart perhaps have a desire to put something back into the sport and find this easier working through a responsible organization. But surely the vast majority of people join clubs because membership means meeting and sharing experiences with other enthusiasts.

Falconry gatherings are true social events. They offer a chance to catch up on the latest news or intrigue and, for the shameless, tell a few fishing tales! Such get-togethers are enjoyable even out of season, but nothing really matches a practical hawking meet and all that goes with it.

In parts of continental Europe, some truly spectacular field meetings are staged and some of the most successful of these are held in Austria by the Österreichischer Falknerbund. These meetings seem to have all the right ingredients in all the right measures: a degree of formality, excellent organization, and a band of people who want to do some serious hawking.

Perhaps the best field meetings of all are held in eastern Europe, and participation in these meets is a wonderful experience. Czechoslovakia is host to the largest meetings, and these attract some of Europe's most respected and accomplished falconers. The emphasis is on hunting and standards are high. Although a variety of birds are flown at these meets, goshawks always play an important role—and this is a hawk the Czechs know very well indeed. Czechoslovakia also draws the golden eagle enthusiasts. In fact, nowhere else are so many hunting eagles regularly brought together.

Typically, these gatherings run over a four-day period, with the first day being set aside as arrival and registration day. This is really essential when one considers just how far some falconers must travel. In years gone by, the journey from western Europe was something of an experience in itself. Then one was traveling behind the Iron Curtain into the Eastern Bloc, and at border crossings one was very much aware of it. There were never any problems, but as one can imagine, a minibus crammed to bursting with people, assorted falconry equipment, and hunting birds tended to arouse a certain amount of curiosity.

Although there is no hawking done on the first day of these meetings, it still pays to arrive early. Everything operates on a first-come first-served basis. Take the hawk weathering area for example: this will be laid out, but some spots may be better than others, offering perhaps more shelter and privacy. The weathering area is of course, each falconer's first port of call. Birds are unloaded, settled in, and offered a bath. This done, it's time to register, pay one's fee, and find a room.

Back at the weathering area, more falconers will be arriving and the place is normally a hive of activity. There are friends to be greeted, tales to be told, and the competition to weigh up. There is definitely an air of friendly competition at these meetings, and birds which have a reputation for being top field performers will be noted.

The following day sees the start of the meeting proper and, after breakfast, falconers collect their birds and assemble for the customary greetings and official opening speech or speeches. Then it's off to the hunting grounds to get down to some hawking. The birds are normally divided into longwing, goshawk, and eagle groups, each group being taken to an area where the quarry and landscape most suits their needs.

The eagle owners come primarily for the brown hares and, when supported by a good number of beaters, what an impressive sight these hare-hawking groups make. Lined up and fairly evenly spaced, a big group can take in an enormous amount of country. Hawking in these eagle groups is fairly straightforward, but the falconer does need to exercise a degree of caution and restraint. The basic principle is, as the line moves off across country, to keep as straight as possible, and one only slips at hares which get up more or less directly in front and ignores those which appear too far to the left or right; these will be flown at by the next falconer. If one is careful, then there is not a lot of room for error. Nevertheless, mistakes in slipping can occur, and for this reason it is far safer not to mix groups (such as goshawks and eagles) but to keep the eagles separate. I remember all too vividly nearly killing Wilhelm Pokorny's gos at a meeting in Austria. Eagles had been given the all-clear and I slipped my bird at a hare I considered to be legitimately mine. Unfortunately, Wilhelm also slipped his gos and, in the ensuing confusion, the hare escaped and the eagle grabbed the hawk. Incredibly, we managed to save the gos, but it was a close call. Of course, if two or more golden eagles pile into the same quarry, there can also be serious problems, especially if a female is involved; but this is a less dangerous situation than when a goshawk comes together with an eagle or eagles.

Another simple, sensible rule is that if an eagle is slipped, no others should be flown until the bird, whether successful or not, has been secured. The risk here is fairly obvious. If the first bird catches its hare, any other bird flown might end up joining it on the kill. By the same token, if the first eagle is unsuccessful, then it can become the 'nuisance bird' if another eagle takes quarry before it is safely back on its owner's fist. The procedure is simple. If a bird kills or is being called back to the fist, the line halts and proceeds only when it is safe to do so.

So much for the theory. In practice, it is not unusual to have several eagles in the air together. This can easily happen in a big group simply by two or three hares flushing simultaneously in different parts of what might be a very long line. But this type of thing is far less risky than when two birds are slipped at the same hare.

The best days are had when hawking in sensible and familiar company, and fortunately, more often than not, this is the case. These meetings tend to attract the same people year after year, and so anyone who has a reputation for being a bit 'trigger happy' can easily be avoided. If one chooses a position among trusted friends or associates and flies with care, then some terrific sport can be had in a big hare hawking group.

I have never kept a hawking diary as such, but over the years have endeavored to jot down a few rough notes during each season. Looking back over my difficult-to-decipher scribble, I am reminded of a very enjoyable Czech meeting in 1986. It was a unique meeting in that it gave me the chance to see a bald eagle flown at quarry. The eagle, an immature male, had been brought along by an Austrian falconer as a last-minute substitute after he had lost his golden eagle to the dreaded power lines. The bald eagle had never been trained for hawking, and at the time was being flown at a falconry center in Austria. There he was encouraged to 'fish' tidbits from the surface of a pool. Indeed, prior to the official opening of the meet, the bald eagle was put through its paces across a nearby lake. We had done the same kind of thing at Schloss Rosenburg and, if nothing else, I knew that a fit male bald eagle could certainly fly. But with fifteen golden eagles and a Verreaux's eagle at the meeting, the bald eagle was in pretty formidable company.

Like everyone else, I was very keen to see just what the bald eagle would do when confronted with quarry; out in the field, my curiosity was soon satisfied. After an unsuccessful flight or two with my own eagle, I watched the bald eagle take on a hare at extremely long range. He caught the hare up with ease, but instead of simply subduing it, he tried to sweep it into the air. He didn't seem to reduce speed at all, and was obviously trying to 'fish' the hare from the field. It all happened very quickly, and almost immediately the eagle lost its hold or released the hare and returned boomerang style without pausing to his owner's fist. Sadly, the bald eagle never did bag a hare, but its presence at the meeting certainly added a dab of color.

Not all Czech falconry meetings have been on a grand scale. I recall a smallish get-together at Choltice, which was to prove, for me, a rather painful experience. The weather for this meeting was very hot, and this made traversing the vast open country hard going. Shade was practically nonexistent, and the only suggestion of moisture was the perspiration oozing from one's body.

One or two meeting officials had arranged for a horse-drawn carriage to take them into the field. Following as closely as dirt tracks would allow, the driver would, very obligingly, periodically relieve the more weary hunters of their slain quarry. This thoughtful gesture nearly resulted in my spending the rest of the season on crutches. During a midday break, I went over to the carriage to deposit two hares. Unfortunately, the driver had not seen me and pulled away, going over one of my feet in the process. Typical, in all that open country, I manage to get run over by a horse!

Hungary is another country where some fine field meetings are held, and the 1991 international meeting was a most enjoyable affair. I attended this meeting with Josef Hiebeler and Jürgen Färber. We arrived from Austria on the sixteenth of October, which gave us time to settle in our eagles before the official opening of the meet on the seventeenth.

The meeting was international in the true sense of the word, with falconers from Austria, Germany, Italy, Yugoslavia (or what was then Yugoslavia), Russia, and, of course, Hungary. The hunting birds included a good number of goshawks, seven golden eagles, a variety of long-wings, and one red-tail.

On day one in the field, conditions were nearly perfect for the eagle group. There was perhaps just a little too much wind, but certainly nothing to moan about and nothing to really hinder hawking. There were plenty of hares and some nice flights were seen. Sadly, two falconers decided to call it a day quite early on, as their birds were just not performing. This made what was already quite a small eagle group even smaller—but I heard no one grumble about this. By the end of the day, all of the remaining eagles had taken quarry. But back at base, the talk was not of the many hares that had been caught; it was of the fox which got away—what was I saying about fishing tales? I still don't think anybody really knows just what happened with the fox flight. There was cover, there was confusion—my bird had hold of it, then Jürgen's, but still the fox had escaped.

Day two was a bit of a disappointment. Hares were very thin on the ground and I believe only three or four were taken by our entire group. However, without wishing to be too critical, we did, at our guide's request, spend the morning in country which seemed rather unsuitable for hares. To top it off, by late afternoon heavy rain set in and the outlook for the following day was none too good.

Day three, the final hawking day, was very wet. It had stopped raining, but ground conditions were far from ideal and we were hardly an enthusiastic-looking bunch as we assembled for the morning lineup. Yet, surprisingly enough, from this rather unpromising start, my two colleagues and I were to end up having a most enjoyable day.

On the way to the hawking grounds, we got separated from the rest of the eagle group, and although we tried (with the help of one of the organizers) to find the main party, we drew a blank. So, with a Hungarian guide and a small band of enthusiastic beaters, we decided to go it alone.

As we lined up to walk a very promising looking piece of ground, I must confess I felt quite optimistic. The weather had become quite pleasant and all three eagles seemed keen to hunt. The first hare was put up near me. A nice flight, swinging left, but the eagle missed. However, I didn't have to wait long for my next hare, and this was taken.

In the open, flat country we were hawking over, roe deer were quite abundant. They were lying out in the low, patchy ground cover but, in the main, they were getting up too far away for a serious hawking attempt. But luck was to be on our side. One roe left its departure a little too late. It flushed to the right of Josef, and his eagle took it in fine style.

Jürgen wasn't having much luck. He was getting the flights, but his rather inexperienced bird simply wasn't making contact with her hares. She was certainly trying and had done well enough on day one, but, now for some reason, things were just not coming together.

This last hawking day had been a relatively short one, due to the initial problem of getting lost, or left behind, and the need to return early for an official gathering. Nevertheless, we saw plenty of fine sport and, with five hares and a roe deer, we were more than happy.

Back at base, we discovered that the main eagle group had also enjoyed a successful day. They had accounted for a number of hares, but their sport was marred when one of the eagles killed Mrs. Bechtold's peregrine. She had gone along to beat for the group but, unwisely, and against all advice, took her falcon along. Returning to its owner following an unsuccessful flight, a male eagle veered off and took the unhooded and somewhat restless peregrine from the lady's fist.

But on a lighter note, as can be imagined, these meetings are quite an event for the local community, and so several open-topped, horse-drawn carriages had been organized to take the visiting falconers and their birds on a round trip of the small nearby town, a kind of grand finale to the meeting. It really was all very peculiar, especially as it was teeming with rain. I was absolutely soaked to the skin and, to make matters worse, as I sat there looking like a drowned rat, Josef's bird lifted its tail and added a large splash of color to my rather drab attire.

Before concluding this look at field meetings, I would like to return to Czechoslovakia and give an account of the 1992 international meeting in Opocno. Meetings at Opocno are the most important on the European falconry calendar, and they are always very popular. The 1992 gathering was no exception, with falconers from Austria, Germany, Poland, Hungary, France, Belgium, Croatia, England, Wales, and, naturally, Czechoslovakia attending. They brought a variety of hunting birds with them, including sparrowhawks, goshawks, sakers, peregrines, gyrfalcons, hybrid falcons, one red-tail, and no less than twenty-eight golden eagles.

Once again, I attended this meeting with hawking partner Josef Hiebeler. Jürgen Färber was also there to make up the team but he had traveled much earlier and had spent two weeks hawking with a Czechoslovakian friend. Between us, we had three male eagles.

Among the many familiar faces at the meet, there were many which were not so familiar. I was very surprised to meet four members of the Welsh Hawking Club. They had decided to take advantage of their invitations to attend the twenty-fifth international meeting at Opocno. None of them had been to a meeting in Czechoslovakia before and they couldn't have wished for a better introduction. They had traveled over in a huge motor home, or camper, which seemed to be equipped with just about everything one could want and more. During a break from hawking on our first day in the field, the camper was acting as mobile canteen, serving up coffee and rice pudding. With all of us huddled round the doorway, from a distance it must have looked like a lunch break on a film set.

Also attending Opocno for the first time was Graf Leonhard Colloredo-Mansfeld. The family Colloredo-Mansfeld had once owned the magnificent schloss at Opocno, which, at one time, was famous for its horse breeding. It was at the schloss each morning that the falconers assembled before heading out to the field.

For hawking, the various hunting birds were split up into groups, falcons, goshawks, eagles—with so many eagles in attendance, these were sent out in two groups. On the first day out, our group, with thirteen birds, found conditions very much to our liking. The area around Opocno is famous for brown hares and over the flat, open country, flight after flight was enjoyed; indeed, the action seemed almost non-stop. The eagles themselves varied in age and experience from first-year birds like the one I was flying to a sixteen-year-old female.

It was during that first days hawking that my eagle was nearly hit by a car. It was at the very end of the day and the hawking line had broken up with falconers dotted here and there ready to return to the nearby vehicles. A fairly casual atmosphere prevailed. Most of the eagles had taken quarry, their owners were tired and things were slowly winding down. Somehow I found myself ahead of what was left of the main group and I turned round to wait for them. All day the country had been of a relatively even nature but now to my left was a small isolated grassy hill with a few stubby trees sprouting from it. Over this, I caught a glimpse of an eagle. It was soon gone, but whoever was up there with their bird had either slipped at a hare or simply disturbed one, as a big brown hare was set on a course which would take it right past me. To avoid my eagle having to take the hare on at an awkward angle, I waited for *lepus* to pass me before slipping. With its hood removed, the eagle was away in an instant and the hare, who was already moving quickly, changed gear to meet the challenge. I can see it all now as if it were yesterday. I remember the thrill, the tension, and the anger as some fool decided to let their eagle go too. Luckily for me, this second eagle made a single half-hearted attempt and was out of the action. My bird stayed with the hare trying to get to grips with it as it ran along a smooth wide agricultural track. It was about now that I became fully aware of the open country road which the hare seemed intent on crossing. The road had seemed so far away I don't think any of the group had seen it as any kind of risk, but as this very long flight continued, I was becoming concerned. A little earlier, I had noticed or half noticed perhaps three cars on this road. Now I noticed a fourth and its speed and direction put it on a collision course with hare and eagle. You could almost hear everyone in the field take a gasp of air as the car hit the brakes and the hare and eagle dodged in front of it. The flight continued on the other side of the road but the hare escaped. The eagle was retrieved safe and sound and the car continued, with a no doubt somewhat shocked driver, on its journey. The incident made an interesting, if for me a rather unnerving, end to the first day. But to get back to the meeting in general.

That evening, after returning the birds to the weathering area and getting cleaned up, Josef, Jürgen, and I decided to track down the Welsh Hawking Club members. We found then at Hotel Opocno, living in the same sort of luxury they were traveling in. The wine flowed and a good evening was had by all.

Day two was a relatively short one for our group, but,

125

nevertheless, quarry was once again abundant and we managed to account for a respectable number of hares and a roe deer. The deer was flushed from a ditch and taken by a male eagle. It was a nice flight, across open ground and, coming late in the day, seemed a fitting point to call a halt to things.

Day three began with a flying display for people living in the area. This always goes down well, especially with the children. Three or four goshawks were flown, a couple of sakers, and three golden eagles. Strangely enough, during the demonstration, a hare got up in the middle of the flying area—it was not flown at.

With the demonstration over, it was time to head out to the field for the last of the hawking. Of the three days' hunting, this was perhaps the most interesting. Interesting because, although hares were plentiful, I don't think I can ever remember an eagle group experiencing so many near misses. At the same time, we certainly saw by far the best flying. Just about every kind of flatland flight was witnessed, and some of the action was truly spectacular. It made the perfect end to a truly marvelous meeting.

8 Ferrets and Ferreting *to* Hawks

When one considers how important the rabbit is to modern falconry in Britain, the ferret's true value becomes clear. This little animal is indispensable. Yet many rabbit hawkers decline to keep ferrets, much preferring to rely on the services of a dog. I can certainly sympathize with this, but the best of hawking dogs can only find and flush rabbits if they are lying above ground; all too often, as the ferretless falconer will discover, they are not.

In addition to those falconers who will simply not keep ferrets, there are others who do keep them but grudgingly. For these people, ferrets are simply a means to an end, or are perhaps seen as a necessary evil. Such falconers are really missing out, for to truly appreciate ferreting to hawks, one must first like ferrets in their own right. In fact, all good ferreting starts at home with happy, healthy ferrets.

Housing

If you care about your ferrets, then their physical and mental well-being should come first. With this in mind, accommodation is something which deserves careful consideration. My own preference is for a spacious outdoor 'court,' or compound. How large this is will depend on the space and resources available. A converted garden shed with an outdoor run is another housing possibility; one friend modified a brick outbuilding, turning it into an excellent ferret court. Such setups have numerous advantages over a more typical hutch arrangement. First, the occupants have plenty of room for exercise, and the need for space becomes obvious when one watches young ferrets during a frenzied play session. With them springing and leaping about all over the place, every inch of floor area seems to be used up.

Perhaps the biggest point in the compound's favor is that one can spend time with one's ferrets, regardless of weather conditions. I think this is most important. With young or new ferrets, these visits give the keeper an opportunity to notice any particular personality traits. Some ferrets will be outgoing and bold while others, for some reason, may be more reserved or even nervy. An individual that tends to run for cover when faced with something new, or becomes startled at some unknown sound, is obviously not ideal material for the rabbit hawker. Among other things, these jumpy characters often prove to be 'skulkers,' dithering about just inside rabbit holes, too suspicious to come out into the open. Such a ferret compares very poorly with the bold adventurous type that simply takes everything in its stride.

Ferrets really do vary a great deal from one animal to another. For example, at the present time I have a four-year-old jill (female) who has always had a passion for climbing up the outside or, if she can, the inside of trouser legs. As a result, wellingtons have to be worn in the compound, or trousers tucked into socks. She means no harm, but it can be a little disconcerting—especially if one is not used to it; and she seems to be able to sniff out an unsuspecting victim very quickly indeed. About twelve months ago, an elderly lady and longstanding friend of the family asked to have a look at the ferrets. We entered the compound and before I realized what was happening the 'trouser ferret' had climbed up my visitor's woolly stockings and was disappearing from view. It was most embarrassing. There was this poor woman dancing round the compound in total panic with me trying to get my hand up her dress!

A ferret compound is a housing option not open to everyone; for some a hutch or hutches need to be used. Some ferret keepers actually prefer to keep their animals in hutches, but now I would only use them when absolutely necessary. A sick ferret is obviously better off quarantined in a hutch. This not only removes any risk to the other ferrets but also makes monitoring its condition and what it is eating (and passing) much easier. In the past, I have also confined the odd newcomer to a hutch within a compound, to try to effect a gradual introduction. A further point for consideration is breeding. With some established communes, there are few problems. With others, the opposite may be true, and then a hutch or hutches will be required.

If a hutch is to be used then it must be as large as possible. For two ferrets, a structure measuring four feet by two feet by eighteen inches high would, in my opinion, be the minimum requirement. The front of the hutch should be wire mesh (square weld-mesh) for about three-quarters of its length. The remainder is better off blanked in, giving the occupants privacy and shelter from the elements. I do not favor built-in nest boxes, but equip any hutches I use with removable ones. This aids hygiene and makes giving the hutch a really thorough cleaning out easier. Having said that, I do not wish to imply that ferrets are dirty animals;

they are not. In fact, they are remarkably clean and instead of completely fouling their hutches the way some small animals do, they use a specifically chosen 'latrine corner;' a generous dollop of absorbent material (wood shavings, sawdust) here ensures daily cleaning out is a quick and simple affair.

Going back to nest boxes, plenty of bedding should be provided, and this can be in the form of straw or hay. Hay has the disadvantage of holding an awful lot of heat and so should be used sparingly or not at all in the summer.

If the hutch is front-opening, then care must be taken not to let any young ferrets fall out. This can happen more easily than one might imagine. An opening roof is perhaps a better option and, if the hutch is outdoors, this will need a generous overhang and be well felted to keep out the rain. It is most important that the hutch is kept dry, the hutch floor especially so. If not, foot and general health problems are to be expected. Placing the hutch under a lean-to is a good idea, and in summer a shady spot is essential as ferrets succumb quite easily to heatstroke.

A final word on housing, whether a hutch or compound is being used, it must be totally secure. Ferrets are top-class escapologists and the very last thing the hawk keeper wants is a loose ferret on the premises.

Feeding

Supplying ferrets with the right kind of food is as important as providing them with the correct type of housing. Sadly, it is still possible to find ferrets being kept on a diet of bread and milk. This is totally unnatural, as ferrets are carnivores. I tend to feed a fairly varied diet, which includes dead day-old cockerels, rabbit, the odd squirrel, and some raw green tripe. I am fairly generous ration-wise, but take care that no excess food is being stored away. Fresh water should always be available.

The Ferrets Themselves

From a working point of view, jills are normally recommended, and the smaller they are the better some people like them. But jills are not always preferred. Hobs (males) are quite popular with some falconers, and I frequently use one myself. If smallish, a hob can be excellent for bolting rabbits. Often just his presence in a warren seems to have the occupants ready to abandon ship.

Whether jills or hobs are chosen, the best plan by far is to purchase youngsters from a reputable breeder. Any plans to acquire working adults should, in my opinion, be abandoned. A good-working, nice-natured 'bolter' is worth its weight in gold to a serious rabbiter, and although adult ferrets are frequently offered for sale, the chances of getting just what you want are slim.

If jills are being kept, then the question of whether or not to breed from them will eventually need to be considered. The biggest worry with breeding is trying to ensure all the kits go to first-class homes. Unless they go to friends, how can one be sure? Also, quite apart from the ferrets' welfare, I am not keen on having strangers call at the house. It is a sad fact that ferret, hawk, and hound keepers need to be very security conscious. With these two points in mind, I would rather buy ferrets when required.

I normally keep three jills and a hob, and find this number of ferrets more than adequate for my requirements. A hob that has been vasectomized is a great asset, for although there is no danger of pregnancy, he is able to bring the jills out of season. If jills are not mated, they stay in estrus throughout the breeding season. With her vulva remaining enlarged for this lengthy period, an unmated jill would be susceptible to infection.

In addition to the choice between sexes, there is the question of type. Ferrets come in a variety of colors but for practical purposes they are normally referred to as being albinos or polecat types. The albino is very distinctive with its pink eyes and white or creamy white coat. Dark polecat types more closely resemble the true wild polecat in coloring and carry similar facial markings.

Although I have successfully used all kinds of ferrets with hawks, falconers are normally advised to choose albinos, as their coloring helps the hawk accept them more quickly as an ally; the importance of this cannot be stressed strongly enough. To go out rabbiting with a bird that obviously regards ferrets as food is asking for trouble. Under such conditions, even an experienced falconer can never guarantee the ferret's safety. Once the bird is slipped, the matter is quite literally out of his hands; it is strange how even the simplest, 'safest' flights can take an unexpected turn. To illustrate this point, I would like to give a simple example. A largish but isolated warren is selected and a ferret entered. As there is quite a distance to the nearest cover, the falconer stands well back and waits. A rabbit bolts and immediately the hawk is slipped. Alas, the rabbit is in view but briefly before disappearing down another hole. The balked hawk might have landed on the ground, but in this instance she goes into a conveniently placed tree. In a flash, another rabbit bolts, but again quickly vanishes below ground; but the hawk is already on her way and, as the ferret surfaces, she has it.

If, as soon as the hawk had missed the first rabbit, a dummy or dead rabbit had been thrown down for her, the flight might have had a less tragic ending.

In truth, there is really no way to bolt rabbit for a bird that is intent on killing the ferret. Even when a rabbit bolts cleanly, if the bird misses and lands nearby she could still possibly get to the ferret before the ferreter or falconer; if this dangerous game must be played (and who in their right mind would want to), then a dummy rabbit must always be kept in readiness as a safeguard.

If gone about sensibly, ferreting to hawks can be exhilarating stuff and is certainly not, as one ill-informed ferret enthusiast wrote, "heavy on ferrets." Nevertheless, no matter how steady a hawk seems with ferrets, I always try to avoid deliberately tempting fate.

Practical Ferreting

If ferrets are being kept for rabbiting with nets, then a list of the equipment necessary for practical operations might prove quite extensive. Much will depend on who is compiling the list and who has to carry the gear into the field. The falconer, especially when working alone, will tend to pack the basics and pray. A box to carry the ferret or ferrets in is fairly essential and this should be made as light in weight as possible—on a long day, every ounce counts. Plywood is very suitable material to build from and, of course, the dimensions of the box will vary according to how many ferrets are going to be transported. A box measuring twenty inches long by eight inches by eight inches will be adequate for two jills. This should be partitioned in half across its width and have a split lid. This means one has two separate compartments, allowing the removal of one ferret without the other climbing out too. The box must be well ventilated with air holes and, for each field trip, contain a suitable amount of bedding.

For any kind of ferreting, a spade is a must. One hopes

it won't be needed—but just in case. An electronic ferret locator is another essential item, and if one of these is deemed unnecessary, then the spade may as well be left at home too.

Perhaps a few words about ferret locators would not be out of place. The principle is quite simple. The ferret carries a small transmitter on a collar around its neck. This emits a signal which can be picked up by a hand-held receiver. The locator I favor is made by Debens and is marketed under the name of 'Ferret Finder.' This locator is very accurate and extremely easy to use. By sweeping across the surface of the warren with the receiver on maximum, the ferret's approximate location is revealed by a distinct intermittent 'dotting' tone. The receiver is then gradually turned down until the ferret is pinpointed exactly. As the volume control on the receiver is marked off in feet (one to eight or one to fifteen) the ferret's exact depth as well as position is known.

Before the days of electronic ferret locators, the traditional way of locating a ferret with a kill was to use a line-hob. He was sent in pulling a line marked off at yard intervals. His job was to find the ferret, drive her off the rabbit, and then stay with it until he was dug down to. Of course, locating the line-hob was hardly a straightforward affair. It was very difficult to judge how far he had gone simply by measuring the yards run off on the line; the tunnels of a rabbit warren do not simply go in one direction. What was required was a combination of listening at the ground, probing along tunnels with a flexible stick (to check direction), and digging the odd inspection hole. Line-hobs are still used by some ferreters, but personally I am quite happy to rely fully on modern electronics.

The rabbit hawker should view digging very much as a

last resort, and every effort should be made to avoid subterranean problems. Silence is of paramount importance, but it's surprising how many people forget this once a rabbit bolts and the hawk is after it. When hawking in a group, shouts and cheers often accompany the pursuing hawk and convince any rabbits still at home that they are better off staying put and taking their chances with the ferret.

If operations can be conducted without a hullabaloo, there is not only less risk of the ferret killing but also the chance of another flight. Should the hawk miss the rabbit, it might be possible for the falconer to speedily recover the hawk and get back into position in case another rabbit bolts. Or, if more than one bird is present, as soon as the first hawk (if it misses) has been secured, another might be given a chance. If the first hawk kills, no other hawk should be flown. The risk here is that the second bird could all too easily end up plowing into the first as it sits victoriously on its prize.

In addition to working as quietly as possible, on a long day the ferrets should be rested or alternated, offered an occasional drink, and at lunchtime perhaps given a bite to eat. The idea that ferrets need to be hungry to hunt is nonsense. Correctly reared and handled ferrets hunt because they love it. However, overfeeding before or during a day's sport is not advisable. Understandably enough, ferrets like nothing more than a nice nap after a real feast. A smallish meal before 'the off' will be sufficient. If taken out hungry, there is far more chance of a ferret killing below ground and staying put with the kill. The well-fed ferret may also kill, but will then tend to move on in search of more rabbits. This does, of course, mean that the odd rabbit will be left underground to rot, which is a terrible waste of good meat, but for the single-handed falconer, this is preferable to digging.

A further point to consider is that there is more chance of a kill below ground when two or more ferrets are working a warren. Because of this risk, I tend to enter just one jill initially and only if the task is obviously proving too much for her do I send in assistance. But the decision to send in another ferret should not be made too hastily. A good jill is a tenacious and thorough hunter, and she may need some time to work a biggish warren; while she is underground, the falconer must hold his position and be patient. An experienced ferret will not normally waste much time on an unoccupied warren, and so if she stays down then the chances are there is someone at home. If she emerges, one should not be too quick to rush over and pick her up. The rabbit she is pursuing may have simply thrown her off the trail for a moment. If this is the case, she will soon disappear below ground again and resume the hunt. Rushing back and forth across a warren will, of course, alert the occupants to your presence.

It might be thought that by using ferret muzzles (which are readily available) one could avoid underground problems, but this is not so. A muzzle might prevent a ferret from killing, but it will not prevent that same ferret from staying with a trapped rabbit a very long time while it tries to kill it. But there is a more serious reason why ferret muzzles should never be contemplated: if a muzzled ferret is lost, its fate is sealed; unable to hunt, it will starve.

Sooner or later, whether precautions are taken or not, the lone rabbit hawker will be forced to take up his spade. One's first priority is to secure the hawk, taking care that it cannot come into contact with anything should it become restless. If the hawk can be hooded, so much the better.

This done, digging can commence. The locator will have revealed the ferret's position, but digging can cause the ferret and rabbit to move, so it is well worth double checking just after work has begun. Also, if I am faced with a deepish dig, I periodically check depth and position. As the ferret's position is neared, it pays to be careful. Overzealous use of the spade might result in the poor creature being injured. On breaking through to the tunnel, it is not unusual to find that the ferret has more than one rabbit trapped up a dead-end 'stop.' Such finds compensate a good deal for having had to dig in the first place. It is worth mentioning that a rabbit sometimes bolts while digging is in progress, and so, if the falconer is not alone, and someone else is doing all the work, he should stay alert.

After digging, any hole or holes should be refilled and, if working on grass, try to replace the turf. Leaving mounds of earth and deep holes in one's wake does not promote good falconer-landowner relations.

Of course, the location of some warrens makes digging impossible. Those built among piles of old bricks and rubble are perhaps the best example, but a warren situated in the base of an old tree can also be a veritable fortress. Large ash trees frequently have rabbits living under or actually in them, but as tempting as these look, they can spell trouble. Although I always try to avoid digging, I never deliberately tackle warrens where digging would be impossible.

If ferreting without a locator or line-hob (and some people frequently do this), then problems underground can be quite serious. With no way of getting to the ferret, one simply has to wait. Calling down entrance holes or rattling a stick inside them can be tried, as can placing a dead rabbit just inside one of the holes (this should be firmly held), but more often than not the falconer will be in for a long wait. Early in the day, this is no great tragedy, but if ferreting has progressed into late afternoon (this is never advisable), then things will look grim. With darkness approaching, one really has only two choices: either block up all of the holes, or block up all but one and, outside this, leave a transport box containing some bedding and food. In both cases, one must return very early next day to either unblock the warren, allowing the ferret to emerge (hopefully), or to check the transport box.

Weather conditions can play an important part in ferreting. The ideal day has been described by some as calm and frosty; but a heavy frost can make a quiet approach difficult. I try not to be a slave to the elements, although I make a point of avoiding windy days. A stiff wind not only makes flights from the fist awkward, but also tends to put rabbits off bolting.

Some fine rabbit hawking is to be had after a heavy fall of fresh snow. If rabbits can be bolted then, such conditions favor the bird, as the quarry cannot propel itself along at anything like its normal speed. This may not be a serious consideration for the goshawker, but the falconer flying a big *Buteo* should not feel too guilty about using the advantage such a setup offers.

An interesting aspect to this type of ferreting is that, due to the deep snow cover, one never really knows exactly where all of the entrance or exit holes are. The ferret enters one of the visible holes and a rabbit explodes in a shower of snow from some previously unseen 'emergency exit.' Open hillsides are the best settings for such flights, but one can experience problems actually getting rabbits to bolt. I have certainly had my share of difficult days in the snow, but the flights are so appealing I can rarely resist the urge to try my luck.

I am sure friend Gary Wall will remember one of our less enjoyable days in the snow, a day which had us nearly expiring from hypothermia on some remote hillside. As we left home, armed with a female ferruginous hawk and two ferrets, conditions seemed near perfect. On the hill, however, visibility was very poor due to mist and beneath the snow the ground was frozen absolutely solid. The lack of visibility certainly concerned me especially flying a ferruginous, but it was to be the hard ground which was, in fact, to create a problem.

Things started off in a very promising way. A suitable looking rabbit hole was chosen and a single jill ferret allowed to ease her way into the narrowed snow-congested entrance. I had already taken up a position some way back, but Gary doing the actual ferreting remained just a little closer to the warren in case the ferret needed to be retrieved or moved to another hole.

The bird I was flying that day had not done much work with ferrets (although totally safe with them) and as a little time had elapsed since the ferret had been entered, her attention had wandered. A slight movement of the gloved hand brought her concentration back into focus and as a rabbit bolted, she left the fist in a very determined fashion. Although definitely hindered by the snow, the rabbit still covered quite some distance (this due largely to my position in relation to the warren) before the hawk sweeping in from behind, made contact with it. The rabbit was taken hard in a flurry of snow but poor footing by the hawk resulted in it being secured only by the lower part of one back leg. The rabbit fought like hell to free itself struggling and jumping, but the hawk held on for grim death and soon had her victim under control. A successful flight but a clumsy display for such a big powerful bird.

So with one rabbit in the bag we moved on, quite confident of seeing more sport. Yet at the very next warren, we encountered trouble. A rabbit refused to bolt and the ferret stayed with it. Knowing the ferret, I realized that the rabbit had got itself into a position where she could not easily kill it. Had the ferret been able to do this, she would have returned to the surface fairly promptly. We (or should I say Gary) decided to dig. It was then our troubles really began. The ground was like concrete and as Gary struggled to make an impact on it, the end of the spade broke clean off! We just looked at each other not knowing whether to laugh or cry. An attempt was made to continue the dig (even using a hunting knife) but eventually we resigned ourselves to waiting. It probably only took something like an hour and a half for the ferret, claws covered in rabbit fur, to emerge, but on that bitterly cold hillside it felt more like three days.

Dogs and Ferrets

If a dog is to be included in a ferreting trip, then it must obviously be rock steady, not only with hawks but also with the ferrets. Personally, I feel that if a lot of ferreting is planned, and not just general rabbit hawking, then dogs are best left at home. An exception would be in the case of a dog which reliably 'marks' occupied rabbit warrens. Such a dog can save a lot of time, for even the most likely and well-used looking warrens can prove rabbitless—and some of the most unlikely looking ones hold two or three. It must be said that a hole-marking dog is of more importance when working with purse nets rather than hawks. If one is going to the trouble of carefully laying nets (and often a good many nets) one really needs to know whether or not a warren is worth bothering with. But the falconer, too, will benefit from the assistance of a good marking dog, especially during an intensive day's ferreting; to actually know as the ferret disappears below ground that a rabbit or rabbits are at home is quite thrilling in itself.

All sorts of dogs can prove capable of marking if given enough field time, but it can be quite a long while before a young dog becomes truly reliable (and some never do). The thing to avoid is encouraging the dog too much. This can create a 'false marker' who will mark each and every warren simply to please its owner. Calm praise is required, but only when the dog is actually marking.

The mark itself varies from dog to dog, depending on the breeding (or crossbreeding) and the individual animal. It might take the form of a definite and typical point, or be little more than a particular stance and expression. Prior to the mark, some dogs will go all light-footed, as if they have sore feet. What is not required is a dog that sticks its head, snorting and snuffling, down rabbit holes. This is totally unnecessary and puts rabbits off bolting.

Once the dog has indicated that a warren is occupied, it should be instructed to take up a position well back and behind the warren. If the dog loiters around the warren, there is a risk of resident rabbits getting his scent, and of him being spotted by any rabbits about to bolt. Rabbits do not always bolt in a fast and furious fashion. Frequently they sit just inside an exit hole for quite some time deciding whether or not to make a dash for it. These are the rabbits that will spot or scent any dog or human who has positioned himself too close. Sometimes when they sense danger, they just sit there, perhaps only a foot or so inside the warren. They may do an about-turn and seek refuge deep in the warren, or they may be grabbed by the pursuing ferret as they sit there. In the latter case, it is sometimes possible to reach in and retrieve both the rabbit and the still-attached ferret.

To be of any value at all, the rabbit hawker's dog must be bidable; and this applies whether it is being used for marking or finding and flushing. A dog which is out to please itself rather than its owner will be more of a hindrance than a help. Yet some falconers won't hear of dogless hawking days and, even when the dog in question is poorly trained, it has to be included. I hate to think how many hawking trips are ruined by uncontrollable canines rushing about and flushing game way out of range. This is infuriating enough when one has no intention of ferreting, but if the renegade dog, or worse still, pack, is sending terrified rabbits scurrying for home, the outlook for ferreting is dim. These terrified rabbits will be most reluctant to venture forth again and, if one is looking for trouble-free ferreting, they are best left in peace. Of course, if several dogs are on the rampage, it is difficult to know exactly which warrens are safe.

It is quite surprising just what sort of behavior some owners will tolerate from their dogs. I remember a fellow falconer inviting me for a day's sport on some ground near his home. Four of us eventually took to the woods with hawks, ferrets, and our host's German short-haired pointer. A suitably located warren was chosen and a ferret entered. A rabbit soon bolted and was well taken by our host's gos. Unfortunately, the pointer had also given chase and proceeded to retrieve both rabbit and hawk. I couldn't believe my eyes, but there was worse to come. The dog relinquished its hold on the rabbit, which our host then stuffed into his hawking bag—with one very bewildered goshawk still attached!

A close friend of mine was to have the pleasure of flying next and, as we moved to another warren, he was literally begging our host to put the dog on a lead. His wishes were complied with and we all felt a good deal happier. Actually, none of us would have continued had the pointer remained at liberty. Our joy, however, was short-lived. As my friend's hawk left his fist in pursuit of the next rabbit, off went the damned pointer too. Its owner had seen fit to release it. The gos was successful and so was the dog, who piled straight in. The ensuing struggle cost the gos four broken tail feathers: more than the pointer's owner bargained for.

Novice Ferrets

Although ferrets do not require formal training, as such, youngsters do need to be brought along carefully and their introduction to rabbiting needs a little planning. Time and care taken in the early stages will pay dividends later.

The ferrets themselves should be from working stock and should have been handled from an early age (as soon as they started to come out of the nest). These things are easy to ensure if one has bred them at home, but not so easy to guarantee if the ferrets are being acquired from another keeper. Hence the need to seek out a responsible and experienced breeder. It is also well worth checking that the youngsters have been fed on flesh.

The need to handle young ferrets from early on in their development is fairly obvious. During a day's hawking, a ferret is continually being picked up, put down, and even handed from person to person. This is only possible if the ferret in question trusts its handler and is 'happy about hands.'

Ferrets are naturally inquisitive, and with young ferrets this desire to explore can be encouraged at home, long before they are taken hunting for the first time. I provide my ferrets (young and old) with no end of artificial warrens, in the form of old boots, lengths of drainpipe, cardboard tubes, and the like. This is very simple to do if one is using a ferret compound.

Patience is required with young ferrets, and initial field trips should be viewed more as learning opportunities for the ferret than serious hunts. Instinct tells the youngster what to do, but practice will be required before it becomes effective at working warrens.

It is very important that the novice ferret is not handled roughly or quickly. If it appears at a hole, it should not be snatched up, but given time to fully emerge. Grabbing at ferrets, young or old, simply makes them reluctant to come quickly out of a warren when their work is done. The same applies when they are required to enter a warren—they should not be forcibly pushed down the nearest hole. If the ferret in question is hesitant to enter one hole, then try it at another.

When to Ferret

It is often said that ferreting should be restricted to those months which carry a letter 'R' in them. I think most experienced ferreters would recommend starting perhaps in October and finishing by March. The earlier one starts, and the later one finishes the more chance there is of the ferrets coming across baby rabbits, which they will kill with little effort.

Early in the season, care should be taken not to leave ferrets in their transport boxes in direct sunshine. As already mentioned, ferrets succumb to heatstroke quite easily and this should also be borne in mind when leaving them in parked vehicles for any length of time.

9 Dispatching and Dealing with Quarry

When it comes to dispatching ground game, it is fairly standard practice to use a blunt-sided stiletto type of knife. This is used either at the victim's head or is pushed into the chest cavity (heart). By using a blunt-sided knife, one reduces the risk to the hawk's feet.

With rabbits, it is also possible to break the animal's neck in the same way as one would after removing it from a net. The back legs are held in one hand and the head is pulled forward and upward with the other. This is a fairly simple procedure when one is standing upright, but, depending upon how and where hawk and quarry are positioned, it can be awkward. And here I should mention that, whenever possible, the quarry should not be moved, as the hawk may well feel it is being robbed. The quarry is dispatched where it lies and is only moved once the hawk has been taken up from it. Of course, sometimes the quarry will have to be moved. A rabbit may be halfway down a hole with the hawk still attached, or perhaps deep in a brush pile, but unless there is a real need to alter their position, hawk and quarry should be left where they are.

When dispatching hares, a method that seems to work quite well (as an alternative to using a knife) is to apply hard pressure to the animal's chest. I tried this for the first time a few seasons ago and found it very effective.

With the quarry dead, the business of taking the hawk up off its kill seems to be a problem area for some novice falconers. Unpleasant scenes are all too often witnessed as falconer and hawk argue over possession of the slain animal. With both parties becoming more and more agitated, what should have been a rewarding and triumphant finish to a flight has degenerated into an undignified tug of war. But then some people seem to care little how their hawks behave on kills. Whether the bird likes it or not, it will be taken up and if this means tempers and feathers getting ruffled, then so be it.

I think many beginners make life hard for themselves by adopting the practice of repeatedly feeding up the hawk on its kills. This is a serious error, for it results in the bird being wrongly educated. Certainly, a young hawk must be satisfactorily rewarded for its efforts, but to continually open up freshly killed quarry and allow the hawk to gorge itself is a mistake. Feed up on a couple of kills, perhaps, but thereafter the bird should be encouraged to accept a substitute on the fist. One's aim is to get the bird into the habit of coming off quarry. This makes life easier when one eventually decides to go for two or more kills per outing.

This business of feeding up on kills is really a matter of common sense. If one is hunting particularly difficult or physically punishing quarry, then the more motivation one can give the bird the better. The rabbit hawker flying an experienced female gos will not adopt a policy of continually feeding up on the first kill of the day, nor will the hare hawker flying a golden eagle.

A sound procedure with relatively inexperienced birds is to make a small incision in the quarry and allow the bird to feed here for a short time before transferring it to the fist; but really, once some degree of success has been achieved, feeding from the kill in this way is unnecessary. This does not mean to say that once a bird has started to account for quarry it should never be fed anything from a kill—it should, but not from each and every one. With young birds, it is a case of trying to strike the right sort of balance until they get into their stride; here, lure work also plays a role. The use of lures or better, lure-carcasses, does not stop just because the bird has begun to hunt; they should be used to bolster the bird's confidence whenever it is experiencing more than its fair share of bad luck.

The secret when feeding a bird from a kill (or training carcass) is not to slit the dead quarry from end to end. If this is done, the bird will be more difficult to take up because, compared with the mass of bloody flesh it has in front of it, a substitute (or to use the correct term, pick-up piece) held in the gloved hand will appear none too desirable. Only a small incision should be made; if a bird is not to be given anything while actually sitting on the kill, then the less blood spilled when the quarry is dispatched the better. Some novice falconers get their birds and themselves into a real mess at the scene of a kill. Blood gets liberally daubed everywhere and by the time the bird has been taken up, the poor quarry looks as though it's been through a mincing machine.

Taking a bird up off a kill is quite straightforward (provided, that is, the bird in question has been correctly handled and trained). First of all, one makes sure that the quarry is truly dead. Until its victim is dead and has ceased moving, the hawk will be most reluctant to come off it. The hawk is then offered a tasty pick-up piece held firmly in the gloved hand, and at the same time one begins to discreetly cover as much of the quarry as possible with a hawking bag. Not until the hawk is on the fist and feeding intently should the quarry be placed in the hawking bag, and this must be done without the hawk being aware of it. I tend to place myself (squatting down or kneeling) between the hawk and its kill. As the hawk feeds on my left fist, I wriggle and slide the quarry into the hawking bag with my right hand. If one has an assistant in the field, then he can simply come in from behind and remove the quarry.

With large quarries (fox, roe deer) a bit of help is always welcome. The bird is taken up in the manner described, but the quarry is simply left where it is. As the bird begins to feed on the fist, the falconer moves over the quarry (again kneeling or squatting), shielding it from the bird with his body. At the same time, an assistant removes or hides the kill, being careful not to let the bird see it. One uses the same procedure when working with large lures or large whole carcasses.

The method I have outlined is not the only way in which a hawk can be taken up from its kill, but it is commonly employed and is certainly the easiest for the tyro to operate. Naturally, some birds are easier to take up than others. By this I do not wish to imply anything physical; I refer only to how willing the bird is, mentally, to accept a substitute or 'reward' for the kill. With furred quarries, goshawks can be extremely obliging in this respect. Harris' hawks require a very careful approach if they are not to show signs of resentment. This intelligent raptor doesn't miss a trick and mistakes made early on will be paid for later. Golden eagles have a reputation for being difficult to take up from kills, but if they have been handled correctly from the word go, they are not.

Once again, it is simply a case of applying a little common sense and adapting to the individual bird. Some hawks will come off quarry (if it is left whole) very quickly for the smallest of rewards, others require a little more encouragement. I watched a chap try to take a male Harris' up off a rabbit using the wing from a dead day-old chick as a pick-up piece. The bird was not at all interested in this meager offering, but the chap persisted (rather forcefully) until his charge was well and truly upset. I suppose that in his mind he was not robbing the bird because he was offering a substitute or reward. But, in truth, he was robbing the bird, as surely as if he had simply wrenched the rabbit away. Would it not have been better for him to present the bird with a more substantial pick-up piece, something more attractive looking, and then discreetly removed this once the bird had eaten what he considered to be enough?

If a pick-up piece is to be removed from any bird so that hunting can continue, it must be done very carefully indeed. As the bird feeds, the pick-up piece is slowly pulled down into the gloved hand, concealing more and more of it. Now, with only a little meat showing, one waits for the bird to take another bite and, as it does, the pick-up piece is placed (now concealed largely in the right hand) in the hawking bag. This does take some practice. The secret is not to rush—a fast, fumbling approach will make the bird immediately suspicious. It all revolves around timing; one has to choose just the right moment to finally remove the pick-up piece. Of course, it helps if one uses a relatively small pick-up piece—the back leg of a rabbit is going to take a bit of concealing. Also, it helps to keep the bird close to one's body, and sometimes it might be found easier and quicker to pop the pick-up piece into a jacket pocket rather than the hawking bag.

Regarding hooding, if the bird is to be hooded, this should not be done too quickly after a kill. Give the bird time to settle down, pick any last morsels from the fist, satisfy itself that the kill is no longer there, and perhaps clean its beak. Then it can be hooded. Hooding too soon can result in resentment. This is especially true with young golden eagles. Having said that, it is possible to hood eagles (without creating ill feelings) actually on a kill, and this is of immense benefit when hawking large quarry. To accomplish this requires very careful training, and the novice would be well advised not to experiment in this direction.

The carrying of dead quarry in the field requires the correct type of bag. Belt-mounted hawking bags might work quite well for falconers who pursue small feathered quarries, but they are of little use when hunting rabbits and hares. The weight of any taken quarry soon becomes an uncomfortable burden when hanging from one's waist. Even a bag carried 'across the shoulder can be irritating unless the strap is nice and broad. The simplest answer is a rucksack. If this is used in conjunction with a more conventional hawking bag, one has the perfect setup.

I prefer not to use bags or rucksacks which are lined with plastic. These may be hygienic and easy to clean, but they are not very 'game friendly.' One wants the quarry to cool down as quickly as possible (especially if destined for the table), and enclosing it in plastic will not help this process. Placing a couple of handfuls of dry grass, or something similar, in the bottom of a standard canvass rucksack will normally keep things fairly clean. I have never considered washing my hawking rucksacks a major chore.

10 One for the Pot

by Carol North

For a long time I resisted eating the rabbits I caught. Cooked rabbit meant scummy stews, head and all, and a far from appetizing smell pervading most of the house. A ferreting uncle bequeathed this image to me along with the stink of badly kept ferrets and the belief that he valued his shivery blue whippet above my Aunt Alice.

Laziness compounded the idea that rabbits were, quite simply, not good eating, as I frequently left the dressing out to someone else. I would then be presented with dirty, gelatinous carcasses with the lower intestine and its contents still intact.

Thankfully I know better now. Rabbit is a tasty, healthy, and versatile meat. But much of the success of a rabbit dish lies in good preparation.

Thorough cleaning and drying, neat jointing, and the removal of unsightly bits of fat or membrane is essential if the dish is to be appreciated by all the members of the family and not only the one who caught the beast.

Clear a working space and have everything at hand before you begin. If you have an outhouse or scullery to work in, so much the better. A table outside will do but flies in warm weather, rain, snow, or freezing hands in winter often make this impractical. If the kitchen is the only available space, clear a work surface and the sink and draining board, as fat and blood have a way of making contact with everything within reach.

The rabbits may have been paunched in the field, but let's assume they are intact.

Have ready a very sharp knife, chopping board, meat cleaver, a hammer or rolling pin, a dish for the ferrets' share, and a large dish for the carcass. Spread several layers of newspaper on the table and cover with polythene or grease proof paper. Begin by pinching the skin just below the breastbone, inserting the knife, and cutting through the skin only along the length of the belly. Pull the fur apart to expose the abdomen. Insert the tip of the knife just below the breastbone and draw it the length of the body, taking great care not to puncture the stomach or the intestines. Take hold of the rabbit around the shoulders and tip the innards into the newspaper. These fall forward when the rabbit is held face down, and all that's needed is a little loosening of the stomach and the separation of the lower gut. Discard this in a layer or two of the newspaper.

The liver and kidneys are now exposed and these can be removed and put into the ferrets' dish. Some people like their rabbit cooked with the kidneys in place, but I always give them to the ferrets as a well-deserved reward. Now puncture the membrane in the chest cavity and remove the heart and lungs, adding these to the ferrets' dish.

To skin the rabbit, begin by cutting through the fur around the throat and chopping the neck with the meat clever or knife and hammer or rolling pin. Chop off each foot at the joint in the same way. Split the head in two and place in the ferrets' dish, but discard the feet as these are of no use. Now force your fingers between the fur and the carcass around the middle of the rabbit. Loosen the skin right around the girth, insert the knife, and cut it into two. You can now take hold of each piece and just pull the skin apart. The front end can be pulled right off, you might have to loosen the membrane a little with a knife around the shoulders of the older rabbit. The hind legs should be eased out, leaving the skin attached at the tail only. Don't pull the skin away here, but lay the rabbit face down on the table and insert the point of a very sharp knife into the backbone a few notches up from the tail. Push through and sever the tail, then pull gently on the skin, cutting through any membrane that doesn't give and you will find that the lower section of the gut will come away with the skin. Needless to say, this method of skinning is no good if you wish to utilize the pelt.

To joint the rabbit, first cut off the hind legs where they meet the back. Now chop the legs in two through the pelvic bone. At this point you can check that all the gut really has been removed. Cut the front legs off by taking hold and lifting slightly, so that the shoulder blade stands out, and cut around this. Next, separate the rib cage from the saddle. I never use the rib cage for anything but ferret food. The meat on it isn't very attractive, and all those bones are fiddly, but it makes a great meal for a couple of ferrets. Finally, chop the saddle into two or three pieces.

Washing the joints is very important, not only to ensure no bacteria from the gut or soil off your hands has contaminated the meat, but also for an appearance point of view. Hold each joint under cold running water and rub off hairs and bits of grit. If the meat is bruised or bloody, soaking for an hour or two in a bowl of cold water will dissipate the blood. Dry the joints thoroughly by patting with a clean cloth, and leave in the fridge at least overnight before cooking. It can be used the same day but seems to improve by being left a while. Do not leave it longer than three days; if you do, freeze it.

Before using rabbit in my recipe, it is important to remove the fine membrane that covers the meat. If it is not removed, the appearance of the finished dish is spoiled, as this membrane either shrinks into a tough band as the meat cooks or turns into a slimy film. Remove it by pinching and pulling and inserting a knife under it. Keep peeling it back and loosening with a knife as you go.

What about days when everything goes right, and you arrive home with a bigger bag than usual? Or the days when everything goes wrong and you arrive home after dark, too exhausted to do anything after settling hawk, dog, and ferrets? Well, rabbits must be paunched soon after killing, otherwise the gut will taint the meat and spoil it for human consumption. But this done, they can be hung. Leaving them in their skins doesn't seem to affect the taste or appearance of the meat at all, nor does it make skinning easier or harder; that depends on the age of the rabbit. In very cold weather, I'm told, they can hang for a week, but I've never left them more than three days. If it isn't so cold, then hang for no more than three days; if it's warm, then do not hang at all. Hang them by the hind legs in a cold room and tie the heads up in plastic bags if there is a risk of dripping. Cutting the throat or piercing the roof of the mouth to allow the blood to drip out whitens the meat. If the carcasses are at all damaged, do not hang, except perhaps overnight, but dress out and refrigerate or freeze.

Damaged carcasses are not at all uncommon when rabbits are taken by any method other than nets. Bruising from shot, talon, or teeth may be improved by soaking as described above, but if it is extensive, then that part of the carcass is best fed to the animals as it creates a lot of scum during cooking and doesn't look or taste good. Many carcasses turn up in the kitchen with a limb already missing, this having been used to take up a hawk from the kill, but as long as you are left with the hind legs, or one leg and the saddle, you can make a meal. A pie can be made with the minimum of meat; just eke it out with veg. You can use meat from more than one animal in a dish, but if you do, use either all young or all old. Young rabbit is very tender and can be cooked in an hour while the most senior member of the warren is only just palatable in four. Mixing them together in one stew creates the problem of the young meat being cooked while the old is still tough, or by the time the old is cooked the young has all but dissolved. This brings us to another aspect of cooking rabbit, how long *do* you cook it? Well, as I've just said, young rabbit cooks quite quickly while the older the rabbit the longer it takes. Three and a half or four hours would be the maximum. The only way to gauge accurately when it is done is by testing. A skewer pierces the thickest part of the meat easily and the bones become loose when cooking is complete.

Because of this variation in the cooking time, difficulties arise with setting mealtimes. Either you must keep your family or guests waiting and watching the clock or you must hope and pray they will arrive early. The simplest solution is to prepare in advance and halt the cooking process if the rabbit is done sooner than anticipated. A stew or casserole comes to no harm if it is removed from the heat and allowed to cool once the meat is cooked. Later, it can be very gently reheated and the finishing touches completed—the thickening, or the addition of cream, parsley, etc.

This problem does not arise with pies, as the filling must be completely cold before it is put into the pastry, otherwise the pastry will become soggy. You can make the filling as far in advance as you like, likewise the pastry, keeping both in the fridge till needed. Time, however, is not the only factor to be considered when cooking rabbit. It isn't simply a case of the older the rabbit the longer you stew it. Temperature is all important. When boiling meat for any length of time, the connective tissue in tough meat is changed into soluble gelatine, releasing the fibers and making it tender in the process. If the temperature is too high, the connective tissue gelatinize too quickly and the meat will be tough and stringy. Once this has happened, no amount of stewing will tenderize it. Very gentle simmering is the key to succulent rabbit. Let the stew come to the boil, skim, and immediately reduce the heat so that the liquid is barely moving—a mere ripple on the surface is all that's needed.

Skimming a stew is well worth taking time to do. Let the liquid come to the boil, lower the heat slightly if it is boiling too vigorously, then spoon off the froth, etc., that rises to the surface. Add more stock to bring the liquid level back up if necessary.

If you have time to make stock, it does enhance the flavor of a dish, so I will begin the recipes with making stock and follow that with the shortcrust pastry.

Stock

4 cups	raw bones
8 cups	water
1 cup	vegetables (onion, carrot, celery, leek)
	bouquet garni*
6	peppercorns

Chop up the bones, removing any fat or marrow. Place in a large saucepan, cover with cold water, and bring to the boil. Skim, turn down to simmer gently. Cover with lid. Add the washed, peeled, whole vegetables, bouquet garni, and peppercorns. Simmer 4–5 hours. Skim and strain.

* Bouquet garni is made by taking a bay leaf, sprig of thyme, and a few parsley stalks, sandwiching them between two bits of celery, and wrapping a leek trimming around this to form a neat parcel, held in place by kitchen string. It can also be bought as a sachet from the supermarket.

Shortcrust Pastry

1 cup	flour
¼ cup	lard
¼ cup	margarine
pinch	salt
2–3 tablespoons	cold water to mix

Sift the flour and salt into a mixing bowl. Put in the lard and margarine and cut into small cubes in the flour. Mix lightly with fingertips until the mixture resembles fine breadcrumbs. Add cold water a little at a time and bind the pastry together using a knife. Kneed lightly until smooth. Leave to rest in the refrigerator for 30 minutes before using.

157

Rabbit and Vegetable Pie

1	rabbit, jointed
1	onion, chopped
1	leek, sliced
1	carrot, sliced
1	garlic clove, crushed
	salt and pepper
	stock
½ cup	mushrooms, sliced
¼ cup	corn flour
1 cup	shortcrust pastry

Place the rabbit in a large saucepan, cover with the stock, and bring to the boil. Turn down the heat slightly and skim. Add the vegetables, mushrooms, and garlic and simmer very gently for 1–3½ hours, until the rabbit is tender. When cooked, remove from the heat. Take the rabbit joints out and remove the bones. Replace the meat. Mix the flour to a smooth paste with a little cold water. Stir this into the stew and return to the heat. Bring to the boil, stirring all the time, and cook for a minute to thicken. Season to taste and leave to cool completely. Roll out half the pastry and line a pie plate. Fill with the stew, dampen the edge, and cover with the other half of the pastry. Make a small slit in the center. Bake at gas mark 5, electric 375°F for 25–30 minutes until golden brown.

Rabbit and Leek Pie

1	rabbit, jointed
1	onion, coarsely chopped
1	carrot, cut into three
1	celery stalk
1	bay leaf
3	peppercorns
2	juniper berries

Place all the ingredients in a large saucepan, cover with cold water, bring to the boil, skim. Reduce the heat and leave to simmer 1–3½ hours until the rabbit is tender. When cooked, remove from the heat and let cool. Then take the meat and remove the bones. Set aside. Strain the stock and reserve 1 cup.

2	leeks, sliced
1	medium onion, finely chopped
2 tablespoons	butter to fry
¼ cup	butter or margarine for the sauce
¼ cup	flour
1 cup	shortcrust pastry
	salt and pepper to taste
1 cup	stock

Saute leeks and onion together, until softened. Make the sauce: melt the butter or margarine in a saucepan, remove from the heat and blend in the flour, return to the heat and cook for 1 minute. Remove again and add the stock, blending well. Return to the heat and bring to the boil, stirring all the time until it thickens; reduce the heat and cook a further 2 minutes. Season to taste. Mix the rabbit, leek, onions and sauce together; leave to cool completely. Roll out half the pastry to line a pie plate. Fill with the mixture, roll out the other half, dampen edge of pie and cover with pastry lid. Make a small hole in the center. Bake at gas mark 5, electric at 375°F, for 25–30 minutes.

Roasted Young Rabbit

1	young rabbit, jointed
2	onions, peeled and roughly chopped
1 cup	streaky bacon
1/4 cup	flour, seasoned with salt & pepper
1/4 cup	butter

Coat each rabbit joint in seasoned flour, then wrap in a rasher of bacon. Coat the bottom of the roasting tin with slices of onion and lay the rabbit joints on top. Cover with the rest of the onion. Dot with butter. Cook at gas mark 4, electric 350°F, for 1–1½ hours, basting as it cooks.

Rabbit and Mushroom Sauce

1	rabbit, jointed
1	onion, roughly chopped
6	peppercorns
1 teaspoon	chopped parsley
	salt to taste
	bouquet garni
3 tablespoons	butter
2 tablespoons	flour
¼ cup	button mushrooms, cleaned and sliced

Place the rabbit joints in a saucepan, cover with cold water, bring to the boil, skim. Add the onion, seasoning, and bouquet garni, cover, and simmer until the meat is tender 1–3½ hours. When cooked, remove the rabbit and keep warm; strain off 1 cup stock. Melt 1 tablespoon of the butter in a saucepan and fry the mushrooms gently for 2–3 minutes. Add the rest of the butter and, when melted, stir in the flour, blend well, and cook gently for 2 minutes. Remove from the heat and blend in the stock. Return to the heat and bring to the boil, stirring. Simmer for a few minutes. Check the seasoning and stir in the parsley. Place the rabbit joints in a serving dish and pour the sauce over them.

Rabbit and Mustard Sauce

1	rabbit, jointed
½ cup	thick bacon, derinded and cut in chunks
2 tablespoons	butter
2 tablespoons	flour
6	onions, coarsely chopped
2–3 cups	stock
	salt and pepper to taste
2 teaspoons	french mustard
	bouquet garni
2 tablespoons	cream
	chopped parsley

Heat the butter in a heavy saucepan and lightly brown the rabbit. Remove and brown bacon and onions. Remove from heat, blend in the flour, then the stock, return to heat, and stir till boiling. Lower the heat, add the rabbit, bouquet garni, mustard, and seasoning. Cover and simmer very gently 1–3½ hours. When the rabbit is cooked, remove to a serving dish. Remove the bouquet garni from the sauce and reduce the sauce over a high heat, until thick, if necessary. Remove from the heat, stir in the cream and parsley, and spoon over the rabbit.

Rabbit in Cider

1	rabbit, jointed
1 tablespoon	oil
2 tablespoons	butter
1 cup	thick bacon, derinded and cut in chunks
2 tablespoons	flour
1 cup	mushrooms, chopped
1 cup	dry cider
2	onions, chopped
1 cup	stock
1	garlic clove, crushed
6	juniper berries, crushed
sprig	thyme
	salt and pepper to taste

Heat the oil and butter in a flameproof casserole and brown the rabbit joints. Remove. Saute the onions, garlic, and bacon until brown. Dust in the flour and cook for a minute, stirring. Gradually blend in the cider, then the stock. Add the rabbit joints, thyme, juniper berries, and mushrooms. Bring to the boil, then simmer 1–3½ hours, until the rabbit is tender. Season to taste.

Rabbit in Beer

1	rabbit, jointed
2 tablespoons	pork fat
1/3 cup	belly draft (pork), cut into chunks
4	onions
1–1½ cups	mild ale
	seasoning to taste
1 teaspoon	sugar
	french bread sliced
	french mustard

Heat the pork fat in a flameproof casserole and brown the pork and onions. Remove from pan. Brown the rabbit, sealing the meat to keep in the juices. Remove from the heat. Pour off the fat and place the pork and onions back on top of the rabbit. Season and sprinkle on the sugar. Spread french mustard on the slices of bread and place mustard side down on top of the other ingredients in the casserole. Pour in the ale, up to the level of the bread. Cover. Cook at gas mark 2, electric at 300°F for 2–3 hours, until the rabbit is tender. Remove the lid for the last 20 minutes to crisp the bread.

Rabbit with Sour Cream

1	rabbit, jointed
¼ cup	flour
2 tablespoons	butter
½ cup	stock
½ cup	sour cream
1 tablespoon	olive oil
3	onions, sliced
	tarragon and thyme to taste
	salt and pepper to taste

Cook the rabbit joints in seasoned flour. Heat the oil and butter in a flameproof casserole, add the rabbit, and brown well. Drain off the fat. Cover the rabbit with the sliced onion, pour on the stock. Sprinkle with a little dried herbs. Cover and cook at gas mark 2, electric at 300°F, for 1–3½ hours, until the rabbit is tender. Stir in the sour cream before serving.

Rabbit Chasseur

1	young rabbit, jointed
2 tablespoons	butter
1 tablespoon	flour
1 cup	stock
1/4 cup	mushrooms, cleaned and chopped
1 tablespoon	oil
2	small onions, finely chopped
1 cup	white wine
1 teaspoon	tomato puree
	bouquet garni

Heat the oil and butter in a frying pan and brown the rabbit. Add the onions and cook 2–3 minutes, dust in the flour, and cook a further minute. Pour on the wine, stock, and tomato puree and blend until smooth. Add the seasoning and bouquet garni, and bring to the boil. Turn down the heat, cover the pan, and let simmer 1–2 hours, until the rabbit is tender. Add the mushrooms and simmer 20 minutes more. Remove the bouquet garni and check the seasoning before serving.

Rabbit in Red Wine

1	rabbit, jointed
¾ cup	thick bacon cut in cubes
¼ cup	butter
1 cup	red cooking wine
1 cup	button mushrooms, cleaned and sliced
1	green pepper, finely chopped
8	button onions, peeled and left whole
3	garlic cloves, crushed
2 tablespoons	flour
	bouquet garni
pinch	mace
1 tablespoon	parsley, chopped

Heat the butter in a large saucepan and cook the bacon until crisp. Remove, add the rabbit joints, brown well. Dust in the flour and cook for a minute. Blend in the wine. Return the bacon to the pan and add the onions, garlic, mace, bouquet garni, parsley, and seasoning. Bring to the boil and leave to simmer for 1–3 hours. Add the mushrooms and pepper, and cook for a further half hour. Remove the bouquet garni and check the seasoning before serving.

Rabbit Stew with White Wine

1	rabbit, jointed
2 cups	carrots, coarsely chopped
⅔ cups	button mushrooms, coarsely chopped
1	leek, coarsely chopped
2	onions, coarsely chopped
3	garlic cloves, crushed
bunch	parsley
2 sprigs	thyme, finely chopped
2	celery leaves, finely chopped
3 tablespoons	olive oil
1 tablespoon	butter
½ cup	dry white wine
½ cup	stock
	salt and pepper to taste
2	large ripe tomatoes, skinned, deseeded and chopped
1	bay leaf
1	garlic clove
2	juniper berries, crushed
2 tablespoons	corn flour

Heat the olive oil and butter in a large saucepan and brown the rabbit joints. Remove to one side. Brown the vegetables lightly, add the garlic and herbs. Pour in the wine and stock and bring to a boil. Lower the heat and add the rabbit joints, chopped tomatoes, bay leaf, clove of garlic, and juniper berries. Simmer for 1–3½ hours, until the rabbit is tender. When cooked, blend the corn flour with a little cold water to a smooth paste, and stir into the stew. Cook a further 2 minutes to thicken. Season to taste.